The Rustling Grass

The Rustling Grass

Joanne E. DeJonge

Illustrations by Rich Bishop

William B. Eerdmans Publishing Company
Grand Rapids, Michigan

Copyright © 1985 by the Board of Publications
of the Christian Reformed Church,
2850 Kalamazoo Ave. SE, Grand Rapids, MI 49560

This edition published 1991 by special arrangement with
the Board of Publications of the CRC
by Wm. B. Eerdmans Publishing Co.
255 Jefferson Ave. S.E., Grand Rapids, Mich. 49503

Printed in the United States of America

Reprinted 1996

ISBN 0-8028-5067-7

Contents

Introduction

If you're not sure that you can really hear God passing in rustling grass, this book is for you. If you are sure — if you think that grass is the most wonderful of God's creations — this book is still for you.

Actually, this book hardly mentions grass. A scant two paragraphs are devoted to that little green wonder. But it does talk about the wonders of that green world, the world of plants. It tells about a skunk cabbage that makes its own heat, a passion plant that begs for attention, and chestnut trees that fight their own battles. It talks about sparkle dust, crowns in oak trees, and plumbing in other trees. It tells you that a tomato is a berry and a sunflower is really hundreds of flowers. It even finds some good in poison ivy.

This book fairly rustles with activity. Cattails pop open, a prickly pear reaches out to touch someone, and a pitcher plant traps its food. A violet makes its own seeds, and a goldenrod makes a home for a fly. Trees bloom, trees fight, and trees close up shop.

This book tells you that you can hear God pass in these rustling activities. He promises another spring as he heats the skunk cabbage. He scatters food when he pops the cattails. He promises new life and new plants when he scatters the sparkle dust, and he reminds us of his very special gift when the passion plant begs for attention.

When you've finished this book you should be convinced that plants don't just sit. You'll know something of their very active lives. And you should be able to hear God passing in the rustling grass.

The Plants and I

When we built our cabin in the woods, I wasn't at all sure what I would do up there. How long can you sit in the woods? What can you do?

So I dreamed up a little project for our first summer: I would become thoroughly familiar with those woods. I would find out which animals lived there. I'd also try to name the bushes they nibbled and the flowers that blossomed underfoot. Of course, I'd figure out which trees grew there and which birds nested in those trees. Oh, yes, and I'd start a bug collection so I'd know the insects that flapped at our screens. And then maybe, if I had time, I'd try my hand at identifying rocks and minerals I found. Since we could go there only on weekends, I figured my project would keep me busy most of that first summer.

Realizing that all of this knowledge wouldn't come to me through flashes of inspiration, I bought a few books — on flowers, trees, birds, and bugs. I

1

figured I would buy an animal book only if I ran stuck. After all, I knew a deer and a coon when I saw one. I could identify a skunk by the smell; I didn't need a book for that. I never bought the animal book, but not because I didn't need it. I was sidetracked and never really concentrated on animals.

I discovered after a few short walks that animals didn't come to me begging to be seen. Quite the opposite; they hid when I came. Within a few weeks I had met some of the bolder ones — squirrels, chipmunks, and raccoons. I had seen deer tracks and had smelled skunk. And I had seen animal droppings (scats), all kinds of them.

I didn't really relish the idea of identifying a creature by poking through its waste. Besides, I discovered that I had enough to do. So I abandoned my list of animals and concentrated on other things.

Sad to say, the birds went next. I knew the ones that came to our feeders. They showed themselves. But the ones in the woods? How could I look down at plants and up at birds at the same time? I considered getting a record of bird calls to help me — after I mastered the bugs and the plants. I haven't gotten that record yet.

I do have a bug collection. It's really an insect collection. I decided to limit myself to things with six legs, or I'd never finish the project. Spiders and other creepers could come later.

A bug collection, of course, goes on and on. A few weekends into that first summer, I realized that I'd never catch one of every six-legged creature in our woods. Besides that, I decided I had to concentrate on one area only.

So I decided to concentrate on plants. They don't run away and they don't bite. They just sit, begging to be identified. When I had the plants named, then I'd go on to the other, more elusive inhabitants of our woods.

Since my project had narrowed considerably, I launched into it with zest. Every weekend I'd troop into the woods, book and magnifying glass in hand, ready to learn more of the plants. Notice that I said "book," not "books." During that first spring there were so many flowers out, I decided to tackle those first. I could always hit the bushes and trees later.

Soon, however, my flower "book" did become "books." My original purchase took me only through June. Different flowers bloomed in July. Later my two books became three. The second book tended to ignore the itty-bitty things. Three became four because number three didn't seem to cover everything either.

Four almost became five. Nothing listed grasses completely. Do you realize how many different kinds of grasses there are? Instead of buying number five, I dropped grasses from my list. I had plenty to hold my attention.

Every night I listed in my plant notebook new flowers I had seen and identified. I also made a card for my file, listing the dates I had seen the flowers. I figured that if I listed the dates each one bloomed every year, I'd begin to see a pattern. I'd know what bloomed when. That way, I thought, I'd soon be able to name the flowers. Then I'd get to the rest of my project.

When the fall rolled around, I put trees in my things-to-do-next-year category. I was still scrambling for the flowers. The number of different goldenrods had me baffled. The variety of asters almost depressed me. Maybe I'd have to let some of the flowers wait until next year.

That was years ago. We've completed our fifth summer of weekends at the cabin, and I still haven't finished my plant project. At last count I had listed over 150 different flowers. Of course, that doesn't

4

include grasses or sedges, which are a lot like grasses. I've ignored the mushrooms and the ferns. The bushes are still there, but I don't know what they are, and I can't even keep all the oaks separate.

And that's just our section of the woods. Were you to put me down, say, in some tropical country or even some different state, I'd have to start all over again.

I must admit that I was sidetracked at times. I couldn't resist collecting a few insects now and then. And it did my heart good to sit and watch the eagle soar or to try to find the wild turkey nest. There is a

huge scat on one of the trails right now. I wish I knew what animal passed that way. Sometimes I just sit and wonder at how much variety there is in creation.

Sometimes people ask me what in the world I do in the woods. How long can I just sit there? they wonder. Then I tell them about the plants.

Skunk Cabbage

Skunk cabbage — what a name! What kind of plant can that be? It certainly must have been low on somebody's list of favorites to be stuck with such a name. The thought of a skunk is enough to make some people's noses twitch, and the mention of cabbage can tie their tongues in knots. A plant called a skunk cabbage certainly can't be much.

Wait a minute! Don't write off the plant because of its name. Maybe even skunk cabbage has something good about it.

I, for one, love to watch it come up in the spring. When you've lived through a long, cold, gray winter, as we usually do, you welcome any bit of green (or purple or brown) that pokes its head through wet, swampy soil early in spring. I don't care that it's called skunk cabbage; it's there, telling me that spring is on the way.

Actually, what's there isn't the normal "plant" part of the plant, the stems and leaves. The little greenish, purplish, brownish thing that melts its way through the snow is part of the flower. It looks like a thick, curled, somewhat rotten leaf, but it's called a spathe.

The spathe tissue is made up almost entirely of small, separated air spaces, like styrofoam. This makes good insulation for the rest of the flower. That's why it's thick, to insulate — and curled, to protect. It's probably deeply colored to attract any insect that might be about.

Inside the protective spathe grows the spadix, the real flower. It doesn't exactly look flower-like, but then it doesn't act flower-like either. The spadix looks like a short, fleshy club. The flowers are tiny and closely packed on this "club." They're greenish-yellow and definitely not the type you pick for a bouquet.

The spadix sometimes acts more like an animal than a plant since it makes its own heat. Most plants warm up in the sun and cool off as the temperature drops, but not the skunk cabbage. This little flower keeps a nearly constant temperature of 72° Fahrenheit, even when the air around it drops to near-freezing. That's why it's one of the first plants up in the spring. It melts its way through the snow.

All living plants and animals produce some heat when they "breathe." But very few plants breathe so fast that they can warm their flowers almost 40° Fahrenheit above the air temperature, and *keep* them that warm. The skunk cabbage can.

Because skunk cabbage flowers are so warm and

well insulated, they're perfect havens for early insects. Bees that may be out a little early can rest and warm up inside the plant. Some spiders mate there and get a head start on spring. In turn, these creatures help pollinate the skunk cabbage and give it an early start on spring as well.

Some cousins of the skunk cabbage produce a powerful chemical that "smells" like decaying flesh and attracts insects. Skunk cabbage doesn't do that. In fact, that warm little skunk cabbage flower almost smells sweet. The skunk part of its name makes sense only when part of the plant is crushed. Then it has an odor of skunk, rotten meat, and garlic combined. Don't crush the plant and you won't have the odor.

The cabbage part of the name makes sense only when the flower is gone and the huge leaves appear. They're rolled up into green "cigars" at first, and then gradually unfurl into green "elephant ears." They don't taste like cabbage, but maybe they look cabbagey.

The skunk cabbage's "root" is even a little different. It's really a stem that grows underground and sprouts hundreds of pencil-sized roots. Each year's roots grow out and down from the stem, anchor themselves in the mucky soil, and then "shorten." As they contract together, they pull the stem farther into the soil. This makes a skunk cabbage very difficult to uproot.

Because it holds so well in the soil, a skunk cabbage can grow for years in the same spot. Most are five to seven years old before they produce their first flowers. Some skunk cabbage plants may be much older than oak trees, or possibly even older than our old redwood trees.

However, a skunk cabbage surely doesn't arouse the sense of awe that a redwood inspires. In fact, it doesn't inspire many people. That's a shame. Any plant that can heat its flower to 72° Fahrenheit, melt its way through snow, provide centrally heated housing for early insects, pull itself into the soil, and live longer than people is surely some wonderful piece of creation. It deserves a better name than "skunk cabbage."

But then, maybe the name really isn't so bad. After all, skunks are rather cute, and cabbages are nourishing.

Cattails

Cattails. They're those tall plants that grow in marshes and roadside ditches. They have long, spear-shaped leaves and look like big cigars. Everyone knows cattails, right?

Right . . . and wrong. Almost everyone knows what cattails are, but very few people really know all about cattails.

Hardly anyone knows that those big "cigars" are flowers. That's right, they're brown flowers. Actually, each "cigar" is hundreds, maybe thousands, of flowers packed tightly together on one stalk. The individual flowers are so tiny that you need a very strong magnifying glass to see them.

To really know about cattails, you have to understand flower parts and what they do. So a short flower lesson is in order, OK? Here we go.

Flowers have two parts which are very important: the pollen and the seeds-to-be. Pollen must reach the seeds-to-be to fertilize them and make new seeds.

That's how the plant can reproduce, make more plants just like itself.

Sometimes insects carry pollen and help brush it on the seeds-to-be. That's why bees and other insects are so important in our orchards and meadows. Or sometimes wind blows pollen from flower to flower to help fertilize the seeds-to-be. (Some people are allergic to certain kinds of pollen. That's why their allergies flare up at those times of the year when pollen is in the air.)

Any way it happens, it's very important that pollen reach the seeds-to-be. Now, back to the cattails.

Cattail flowers are so tiny that not even insects recognize them as flowers. They have no petals with showy colors to attract insects. They have no nectar that insects like to drink. Insects simply don't flock to cattails.

Those flowers are also packed together so tightly that the wind doesn't often blow them away. It would take a very strong wind to blow cattail pollen from one "cigar" to the next.

So cattails have been given a very special way of moving the pollen to the seeds-to-be. The flowers with pollen are placed at the very top of the "cigar," and the pollen sacs grow out beyond the edges of the flower. The flowers with seeds-to-be are placed below the pollen flowers.

The flowers with pollen become ripe first. The pollen sacs open and pollen falls out. Because the sacs extend beyond the flower edges, the pollen falls down and lands on the flowers below. These are the flowers with the seeds-to-be. They open a bit, and the pollen settles in and fertilizes the seeds-to-be.

Cattail pollen, by the way, is water-resistant. If you throw the pollen into water it will float. Somehow each grain of pollen wears a kind of raincoat that sheds water.

Do you know *why* that must be? Just look at a cattail, or imagine one. That "cigar" stands right out in the open for the whole world to see and for every shower to rain on. Wet cattail pollen doesn't do a good job of fertilizing seeds-to-be; dry pollen is much better. Since the whole "cigar" isn't protected from rain, somehow the pollen grains are. When rain falls on a cattail, the pollen grains will shed the water.

Soon after the top flowers have shed their pollen, they wither and fall from the stalk. Their job is done. You can see where the pollen flowers have been on any brown cattail. Look at the very top of the "cigar." Do you see a piece of bare stalk? That stalk used to hold the pollen flowers.

After the seeds-to-be receive pollen, they become tiny seeds. They're microscopic brown nutlets connected to downy hairs.

Most flower seeds need some way to travel away from their parent plant. If they landed right next to the original plant, they wouldn't grow very well, since that patch of ground has already been taken. So they must move away a bit. That's why there are downy hairs on the cattail seeds. When the seeds are ripe, they come off from the plant quite easily. A wind

catches the hairs and blows the seeds away from the original plant.

You can tell when cattail seeds are ripe: the whole "cigar" seems to break apart into a downy fluff. The fluff is made up of thousands of tiny hairs attached to seeds. Look at cattails in late autumn or even during the winter. You won't see a "cigar"; you'll only see fluff.

In fact, any time you look at a cattail — even when you ride past it in your car — you can tell just what the flowers are doing. During spring and early summer, the whole "cigar" will be green instead of brown. All the flowers are developing.

Then for a short time during the summer the "cigar" is brown with a little patch of yellow on top. The pollen flowers are ripe and are dropping their pollen to the flowers below.

Later in the summer the "cigar" will have a stick poking out of the top. The pollen flowers have fallen and the seeds are developing.

During fall and winter the "cigar" will have turned to fluff. The seeds are scattering.

Doesn't knowing all of that make cattails much more interesting to you? And besides being interesting, these plants are also very useful. Because they usually grow in large groups, cattails make excellent nesting places for marsh birds. They also provide shelter for young fish (remember, they grow in wet places); and they provide spawning ground for sunfish. Muskrats and beaver love to eat roots and stalks of cattails. Geese and teal also eat the roots and sometimes the seeds.

Even people eat cattails. It's been said that a person never need starve if there are cattails nearby. The roots are rich in starch and can make a good flour. The stalks, I'm told, can be eaten raw or boiled, like asparagus. Some people eat the green flower spikes as corn on the cob, and the pollen is supposed to be good as a flour.

Besides that, people have used cattail leaves to make baskets and mats and to weave chair seats. The fluff from the seeds has been used in life preservers, or matted down and used as bandages. At one time the fluff was even used in clothing, to replace cotton.

All of that goodness comes from a plant you probably never thought about much. Everybody knows cattails, right?

Not really. But then, most of us don't know many of the common wonders that God has placed at our feet.

Our Sickly Prickly Pear

"Something's been eating our prickly pear," I reported with a wince. I don't know if the wince was for our chomped-on plant or for the animal that did the chomping. Both must have suffered a little in the process.

Why something would chomp on a prickly pear is beyond me. If it were a real pear, I could understand. Put a pear outside near the woods, and something will amble by and pick it up. But a prickly pear? That's a cactus, complete with spines and barbs and all sorts of things that would bite anything that bit it.

You're probably wondering what in the world we were doing with a cactus on the edge of the Michigan woods. Cacti (more than one cactus) are desert plants that belong in Arizona or Texas or someplace like that, right? You're probably thinking that if we were dumb enough to plant a cactus in Michigan, we deserve to have it chomped on. Right?

Right and wrong. Cacti *are* basically desert plants — that's why they're made the way they are. Most of them have tiny leaves or no leaves at all. Leaves usually have pores that lose water, and cacti can't afford to lose water in the desert. Cacti do have some pores — fewer than most plants — but they're usually pressed into the stem. The pit around each pore traps air that traps moisture the cactus shouldn't lose. Many cacti also carry a coat of wax, and some add a layer of hair to trap moisture.

Cactus stems are usually thick and fleshy; water is stored in the stem. The tough, thick skin around the stem traps the moisture inside. And cactus roots are usually netlike. They spread far out from the plant to catch any rain. So cacti can and do live in deserts.

However, the desert isn't the only place cacti live. Some grow right here in Michigan. Two types of prickly pear grow naturally here. In fact, we pass some prickly pears growing in a field every time we go to our cabin during the summer.

We have one sunny spot in front of the cabin, where the soil seems to be well-drained. This is what cacti need. We had already put some hedgehog cacti there. These cacti don't grow naturally in Michigan, but they bloomed in appreciation two weeks after we planted them. So I figured the sickly prickly pear I had cooped up in a pot in Grand Rapids would also appreciate a breath of fresh air.

I had visions of our prickly pear blooming gratefully a week or two after we transplanted it. It hadn't bloomed at all during its five years as a resident of my plant stand. Even if it had, there would have been no insects in our living room (I hope) to pollinate it. It probably would never have made its little berrylike fruit (which really doesn't look like a berry anyway).

Some cacti make edible fruit when their flowers are pollinated. The fruit looks more like another little piece of cactus than a berry, but I'm told it makes acceptable jellies.

Prickly pears, if they don't flower, have other ways of making more prickly pears. A healthy prickly pear looks like a bunch of green, pockmarked, oval-shaped pancakes stacked end to end. When the plant is exhausted and can't grow any more, one of the top "pancakes" falls off. It takes root and starts a new prickly pear. I suppose they're made this way so that they can keep making new plants even when there are no insects nearby.

Our potted prickly pear had tried valiantly to make new plants. Several times little "pancakes" had fallen off and taken root. But there's not much room in a five-inch clay pot.

I suppose the prickly pear's roots were even a little uncomfortable. After all, those roots should spread over a wide area, not just five inches. No wonder it was sickly. I figured it would revive after I planted it outside where it belonged.

You should handle any cactus with care. Most of them have sharp spines. But our prickly pear has no spines; it has sinister little glochids. Glochids look like harmless tufts of downy hair and almost invite an appreciative little pat. Actually, each little "hair" has a tiny fishhook lurking at the tip. If you pat it, it'll grab you and stick tight.

How well I know! When I carried our harmless-looking sickly prickly pear — pot and all — to the car, I think it reached out and touched me. Probably I wasn't looking and touched it by accident; I know we made contact. I sat for thirty minutes with a magnifying glass and tweezers trying to undo the damage it had done to my hand. I didn't mind too much; it was painfully clear to me that our prickly pear had a good defense. It could take care of itself in the great outdoors.

One week after I transplanted the cactus, we went back to the cabin. Immediately I checked the prickly pear — from a respectful distance — expecting to see bumpy little buds. But instead of bumps I was greeted by dents. Not little bug-type chew holes but big animal-type bites. Whatever had chewed on our cactus hadn't taken only one bite to learn a painful lesson. It had come back for more. Three big bites almost did in our little transplant. I didn't think that it would last.

By the next week I was afraid to check the poor plant. Would the prickly pear be chewed down to the roots? Or would some little animal be lying belly-up next to my sinister plant, done in by a mouthful of glochids?

I needn't have worried, of course. The cactus was still hanging in there. It had been chewed on again, but it had started to grow just a little bit.

So it went all summer and well into the fall. Something kept eating the cactus, but the plant stayed alive and even grew a little. Sometimes I worried about it; at other times I worried about whatever was eating it.

I haven't seen the cactus for a few months now. I suppose that it's covered with snow. I'm not worrying about it anymore. I know from painful experience that my prickly pear was created to take care of itself and even make more of itself. Maybe next spring I'll find that it has defiantly dropped a "pancake" to start all over again.

I shouldn't worry about some little prickly-pear eater either. I'm sure the animals around there were created to take care of themselves. If that four-footed cruncher came back for a second helping, a diet of prickly pear must agree with it. Who knows? Maybe there's such a thing as a tough-mouthed, glochid-loving cactus eater, created to munch on prickly pears. If there is, judging from the way most plants and animals are created, my prickly pear and this animal will get along just fine.

Sunflower

Have you ever taken time to really look at a sunflower? I don't mean the quick-glance-oh-that's-a-sunflower type of look. I mean a let's-see-what-this-flower's-like type of look. If you haven't, try it the next time you pass a sunflower. You may be surprised at what you see.

First, look closely at the flower itself. It looks like one huge flower with yellow petals and a brown center, doesn't it? Look more closely. It's really hundreds of tiny flowers (called florets) packed together.

Any one of the florets growing alone, especially a brown one, probably wouldn't attract much attention. Insects would fly past it to bigger flowers. But packed together and rimmed with yellow, these florets almost shout, "Flower here! Come and look for nectar!"

Look closely at one of the yellow "petals." It's really a floret called a ray flower. A ray flower is a tiny flower with a petal shaped like a strap. Because

25

these ray flowers are colored brightly and so many of them rim the "flower," they attract insects to the plant.

Now look closely at the brown "center," or disc. It's really hundreds of floret buds arranged in a beautiful circular pattern. Gradually these florets will open. The buds on the edge open first, followed by those toward the center of the disc.

If one of the florets is open, gently pick it so you can look at it more closely. It is a complete flower. It has tiny petals fused together. Above the petals stands a stigma, the part of the flower that catches the pollen. Below the stigma is a little tube called a style. This leads to the ovary, the place where the seed is made. Besides that, the floret has a stamen with a bit of yellow pollen. Pollen has to land on the stigma to make a seed in the ovary.

All the parts are there in that floret. You're holding a complete tiny flower in your hand. Yet it is just one part of that huge sunflower.

Now step back and look again at what you always thought was one flower. Can you see now that it's really hundreds of tiny flowers arranged into one grand design? Beautiful, isn't it?

And the design works. You've probably already noticed beetles on the "flower." Maybe a bee or two has come in for a landing while you were looking. A butterfly may have alighted for a moment.

All these insects come for a little nectar and perhaps some pollen. As they burrow from floret to floret, they brush pollen onto the tiny stigmas. They

help the "flower" make seeds, and they are rewarded with a little nectar.

If you would come back to this "flower" in about a month, you'd probably see that the center had hundreds of seeds, all arranged in that beautiful circular pattern. Each floret within that "flower" will make its own seed. This one sunflower, because it's really hundreds of flowers, can make hundreds of sunflower seeds.

If you wait too long to return to this "flower" you might not find any seeds. Birds love to eat sunflower seeds. So do squirrels, chipmunks, and people. During nippy autumn days, one sunflower supplies many creatures with food.

Even before the plant goes to seed, it supplies food and protection for many creatures.

Look closely at the leaves and stem, and you'll see what I mean. You may see some aphids, tiny plant lice, anchored to the stem. They stick their little beaks into the stem and suck juices from the plant. Too many aphids may kill the plant, but usually there aren't too many.

See that ladybug walking up the stem? She's the reason there aren't too many aphids. Ladybugs eat aphids. As the ladybug eats, it helps the sunflower. This ladybug may lay eggs under some of the sunflower leaves. She needs someplace to attach her eggs, so the sunflower provides her with the place. The larvae that hatch from the eggs will help the sunflower by eating harmful insects.

Another sunflower leaf is providing shelter for a

spider. She has also laid eggs and enclosed them in a silken ball. Now she attaches the ball to the underside of a sunflower leaf. When the plant dies, the spider eggs will remain attached to the leaf. All winter they will be protected from snow and ice by a dead sunflower leaf. Next spring, baby spiders will hatch.

A grasshopper lands on the sunflower stalk. It sits under a leaf, absolutely still for a moment as a bird passes overhead. The grasshopper's green color matches that of the sunflower plant, and the large leaf hides the insect from the bird. The sunflower has protected the grasshopper.

Some beetles are walking along the stem. Not all beetles come to the blossom. Some suck juice from the plant. Others eat insects that are eating the plant. Still others may have come simply for a rest.

If you could look at the stem with a magnifying glass, you might be able to see a small hole. Sometimes a moth will lay eggs on sunflower stems. The larvae that hatch from these eggs eat their way into the stem. They stay inside all winter, long after the sunflower plant has died. There they are safe from birds, and they have plenty of food. In the spring they change to moths, crawl out of the dead sun flower stalk, and fly away.

This one sunflower plant is a world in itself, populated by more creatures than you'd imagine. Did you ever think, when you walked past one sunflower plant, that you were walking past a whole world?

Now back away from the sunflower plant a bit. Notice where it's growing. It's probably in some un-

29

tended field, or maybe even at the side of a road. The soil is dry and dusty. Animals and people may have brushed by it or even trampled it a bit. Cars may have sped past it, spreading exhaust fumes. No person planted this sunflower. No one waters it or pulls nearby "weeds" to help it grow. Yet it's a hardy plant, growing well all by itself.

Well, not really all by itself. We know that God made sunflowers hardy. And he sends the rain and the sun to help them grow. That's how he provides food and protection for many of his little creatures.

The next time you pass a sunflower, stop and take a closer look. In that one plant you can see hundreds of flowers and a world of creatures.

Indian Pipes

The first time I saw Indian pipes I thought I was looking at a plastic bag. We had just bought our property in the woods, and I was proudly showing it off to someone. We were walking down a well-worn animal trail, and I stooped over to pick up this "crumpled plastic bag." Nobody was going to litter my property! But the "bag" was rooted. I was looking at my first Indian pipes.

You probably wonder how in the world I could mistake a wildflower for a plastic bag. A plastic bag, even crumpled, looks like a plastic bag. Wildflowers generally look like green plants with flowers. But not Indian pipes. They're completely white — waxy white — stem and all.

You see, Indian pipes are parasitic plants. That means they don't make their own food but rely on other plants to do the job. Most plants use their own green chlorophyll to turn sunshine into starch and sugar. But Indian pipes suck up food from rotting leaves and roots. They don't need green chlorophyll, so they're completely white.

Some people don't like any kind of parasite. To them *parasite* means something that doesn't work but lives off something else. But I like Indian pipes for two reasons, even though they are parasites.

First of all, they are delicate, pretty plants. They bloom in the woods in July. Not many other wildflowers bloom at that time. Plants that make their own food from sunshine need sunlight, of course. So they must bloom before leaves are out on the trees. Indian pipes can bloom in the middle of the summer because they don't need sunlight.

In early July, little white knobs push up through the dead leaves on the forest floor. First they look like tiny, waxy mushrooms, but soon the stem stretches up. The stem stands about as tall and as thick as a pencil. It's white and has little "wax" chips instead of leaves.

One small flower forms at the end of the stalk. It looks like a white wax bell with curly edges. The flower droops over, so the "bell" looks as if it's ready to ring.

Sometimes one Indian pipe will grow alone, but usually small groups of six or seven grow together. When I see a group of them with their drooping flowers, I can't help thinking of a small group of people standing in church, bowing their heads for the final blessing.

The "final blessing" in this case is a visit from an insect. I don't know what kinds of insects visit Indian

32

pipes, but I do know that they're needed to help the plants make seeds. After the insects visit and seeds begin to form, the flowers straighten their necks and "look up." That's how you can always tell when an Indian pipe is forming seeds.

When the seeds are ripe, the wax-chip leaves begin to turn black. The head turns black too. So for a while the plant is a stark black and white. Then the rest of the plant may turn brown or black and dry up and shrivel.

In the fall, leaves drop and cover the spot where the Indian pipes grew. But the roots are still there, anchored in the soil. Next July more Indian pipes will grow, nourished by the leaves that fell in the fall.

I'm always tempted to pick Indian pipes when I see them in July. But they turn black as soon as they're picked. Besides that, they're pretty in the woods and they're doing a job.

That reminds me of the second reason I like these pretty parasites. They're using nutrition locked in those dead leaves in such a delightful way. Let me explain this.

When leaves fall from trees, they still contain some good minerals — some nutrition. Somehow, that nutrition must be freed from the leaves and other woodland "rubbish" and returned to the soil. Often, insects, worms, and other little creatures do this work. They chew down the leaves to smaller and smaller bits until plants can use those microscopic bits for nourishment.

Insects, worms, and the like do a fine job of

breaking down leaves and "rubbish," but you don't often see them. They're interesting, but I don't think they're as pretty as Indian pipes.

Indian pipes actually bloom as they work. They use the rotted leaves and help break them down. And the withered stalks of Indian pipes break apart easily. So they're helping unlock nutrition in leaves as they add a touch of "prettiness" to the woods.

So you see, all parasites aren't bad.

If you happen to walk in some woodlot next summer, look for Indian pipes. You may see a touch of beauty that God added to his recycling process.

A Promise in a Bulb

In March, spring is on its way. In fact, the calendar will say that it's here already, although the weather won't always cooperate. We could still get snow in the Midwest, but it won't last long. Milder climates could still turn cold, but they'll warm up soon. Grass will turn green, spring flowers will pop up, and leaves will unfold on trees. Spring is on its way and summer is sure to follow.

The woods around here will be brown and wet and soggy yet. But I know they won't stay that way. In a few weeks they'll be carpeted with early spring flowers. In fact, even in March plants begin to stir. I can't always see them, but I know that they're waking up. They always wake up in the spring.

First, small green leaves will poke up from beneath the dead brown leaf litter. There will be all shapes — long and stringy, broad and pointed, feathery and floppy. Thin, slender stalks will push up and small, delicate flowers will open. The woodland flowers will be the first to bloom. They bloom first every year.

In our woods, a flower called spring beauty will be one of the first to bloom. It won't grow tall, and the leaves will be rather stringy. But the flowers will be beautiful, delicate pink or white heralds of spring. Each spring beauty flower will have five petals, and each petal will have fine pink lines marking it.

Toothworts will probably bloom soon also. They'll look a lot like spring beauties but they'll grow a little bit taller. Their leaves won't be stringy. Instead, they'll be divided into narrow sections with toothed edges.

Dutchman's breeches will soon stir in the breeze. They look like white floppy pants turned upside down on a stalk. They'll poke just a little bit above their soft, fernlike leaves.

Trout lilies will splash the woods with yellow. Each small lily will grow on a slender stalk between two pointed green leaves that are streaked with brownish markings. These lilies won't grow high — just a little above your ankles — but they'll bloom. They do every year.

Other flowers will bloom in our woods also, and different flowers will bloom in different woodlots. But they'll all follow the same pattern. They'll all bloom soon, before leaves unfold on the trees.

Woodland flowers *must* grow and bloom quickly. Many are sun plants; they need full sunlight to grow well. When the trees above them begin to leaf out, their sunlight will be blocked. So they will grow,

bloom, and make seeds before the trees leaf out. Then they'll wither and disappear.

Of course, they won't disappear completely. They'll still live, secretly, in the top few inches of soil. Before their leaves wither, these plants will make food for themselves. They'll store this food in hidden underground stems.

Spring beauties and Dutchman's breeches will store their food in corms, underground stems that look like flattened peas. Tiny buds may appear on the tops of the corms, but the buds will be protected by scales.

Toothworts will store their food in rhizomes, thick sideways-growing stems.

Trout lilies will store their food in bulbs. The underground stem is only a short part at the bottom of the bulb. The food is stored in the thick scales that grow around it. But the whole bulb will be underground.

Other plants will store their food in other ways. But they'll all follow the same pattern. They'll all make food in early spring and store it underground throughout the summer. Using the stored food, they'll send out new roots next fall. They'll even develop new shoots and new flower buds next spring. They do it every year.

Right now these little plants are beginning to stir. Their food has been stored for almost a year. They have lived hidden in the ground, protected from freezing cold and from animals looking for food. Now the corms, the rhizomes, and the bulbs are getting ready to push up new leaves. Soon they'll grow, bloom, and make food. Then they'll wither and disappear again. They do it every year.

In March the calendar says it's spring. Even if the weather doesn't cooperate right then, it will. Soon grass will turn green, spring flowers will pop up, and leaves will unfold on trees. It will happen because spring always follows winter. It will happen because God promised us that, as long as the earth remains, season will follow season. And as a sure sign of that promise, in early spring the corms, the rhizomes, and the bulbs will begin to stir.

A Tomato Is a Berry

"A tomato is a berry; a strawberry isn't." Silence. The conversation had been about legal and illegal fireworks. My mind had wandered off in its own direction and came back with the above tidbit. So I threw it into the conversation, where it was pointedly ignored. I didn't feel like explaining my train of thought to anyone, so I left them with their fireworks and went back to my berries.

A strawberry really isn't a berry; it's a fruit called an aggregate, and so is a raspberry. A mulberry is called a multiple fruit.

And the strangest things are really berries, like tomatoes, green peppers, bananas, and eggplants. Oranges are a special type of berry called a hesperidium; watermelons are special berries called pepos.

You'd think a squash would be a vegetable, but it's a berry. Usually you think of a berry as a fruit. Anyone "knows" that a squash is a vegetable (though a rather questionable vegetable in some young minds).

A lot of what we call vegetables are scientifically classified as fruits. A fruit is really the part of a plant that holds the seeds. So just about anything we eat that has seeds or is a seed is really the fruit of a plant. We just use the word "fruit" loosely, I guess.

I glanced around the yard where we were sitting. The acorns on the oak tree were fruits, I figured; so were the beans and the zucchini in the garden. They all had seeds.

Different fruits have different names, depending on how they develop. I dug back into my memory to drag out some of the names.

Berries are covered with a skin or a rind and have seeds in the flesh of the fruit. That means that grapes are berries, as well as tomatoes.

Apples and pears are pome fruits; the seeds are in a core.

Nuts are one-seeded fruits with hard flesh around them.

Grains are fruits that have seeds fused to hard flesh. Corn is a grain, so corn is a fruit.

A peanut is a fruit, but it isn't a nut type of fruit. It's some other kind. I couldn't dig up the right classification for a peanut. I thought of a cherry, but I couldn't dig up the right name for that either.

I guess it really doesn't matter. We'll still call certain foods "fruits" and certain fruits "berries." A bean will always be a "vegetable" to me, even if it's really a fruit. My stomach won't know the difference. All my stomach will know is that it's food.

My mind suddenly took a left turn and wandered in another direction.

It's really fascinating the way all these fruits develop. They were all flowers once. Some, like squash and pumpkin flowers, were big and showy. Apple and strawberry blossoms are rather pretty and delicate. Oak flowers — yes, oaks do have flowers — are very small.

The beauty of it all lies in the fact that these flowers develop into fruits that we can eat. They're a pretty sight in the spring, some of them smell good, and they're interesting as flowers. Some of them are designed to attract certain insects to pollinate them. Some are designed to pollinate themselves. Some depend on the wind for pollination. But in the end they develop into foods that we can eat. They're useful to us, besides being fascinating.

It's a good thing, I thought, that I didn't have to create the world. I would never have thought of taking something like a flower and making it grow into a fruit for people to eat. If it were left to me, there wouldn't be half as much food in the world. If it were left to the people I was sitting with, flowers probably would develop into firecrackers. I didn't say that aloud, of course; I just thought it.

I glanced at the garden again. Some of the foods growing there weren't fruits. Our little carrots are roots; the seeds grow somewhere else in the plant. The asparagus we eat is the stem of a plant; we don't eat asparagus fruits. Lettuce is leaves, beets are roots. Onions are really specialized underground stems called bulbs. The flower of an onion plant is pretty and you can watch the seeds develop, but you eat the bulb.

The way plants grow really is amazing. We sprinkle a little, weed a little, and expect our garden to give us food automatically. And it does. Those tiny seeds we planted were created just right to develop into all sorts of plants. And the plants that develop were made just right for us to eat the stems or roots or leaves or fruits. All the food we need just springs right up out of the ground. It's almost like magic, but that's the way God created things.

My mind rested for a minute, just thinking about how glad I was that God has created such fascinating plants. What would we do without them? I admitted to myself that my mind is far too small to think of something like making plants for food. I can't even really understand how the plants grow. But I surely am glad they do.

My thoughts turned around once more. What is a peanut called? What is a cherry?

I couldn't remember a peanut at all, but the name for a cherry popped into my head. "A drupe, that's it! A cherry is a drupe." I blurted the last thought aloud, but no one heard me. They were talking about paving the church parking lot.

A Violet Blooms

A violet blooms in the woods, tribute to a Creator's care.

Four years ago, several tiny violet seeds were dropped into the litter on the forest floor. Birds ate some seeds, insects attacked others and still others were dropped where they couldn't grow. One little seed, however, enclosed in a hard shell, remained unharmed and lay throughout the winter.

Spring brought the proper combination of moisture and light, and the seed began to stir. A root reached into the soil, searching for a pocket of moisture. A small stem broke through the top of the soil.

The little plant was tender that first spring. If the sunlight had been too warm, the plant might have withered and died. If the mold that is common on the forest floor had grown around it, the plant would not have survived. But the violet lived and put out three leaves.

Soon leaves appeared on the trees and blocked

45

the sunlight from the violet. Growing ferns and bushes drained water from the soil. The temperature rose, litter on the forest floor dried, and the tiny violet began to wilt and droop. Yet the soil held enough moisture to keep the plant alive.

Summer brought a siege of insect larvae and slugs looking for small plants to eat. Some of those creatures would have found the young violet very tender. But the plant escaped attention and lived through the summer.

During September the three violet leaves turned yellow. The nutrients in the plant moved to the roots and underground stem for winter storage. The small plant formed one terminal bud that could withstand the coming winter.

Early the next spring the little violet stirred again. Created to capture the sunlight between the first spring thaw and the appearance of leaves on the trees, the violet grew rapidly in May. It put out six strong leaves; yet it did not flower.

The little plant was still tender. A hardy fern growing nearby could have choked the violet. A falling branch or the hoof of a passing deer could have crushed it. Yet the plant grew.

For three springs the violet grew but did not bloom. It became strong before it produced seeds.

Now it is the fourth spring and the violet blooms.

Five purplish-blue petals unfold. Two top petals stand straight, or even lean back a little. Two stand sideways, like blue ears. The larger lowest petal tilts forward.

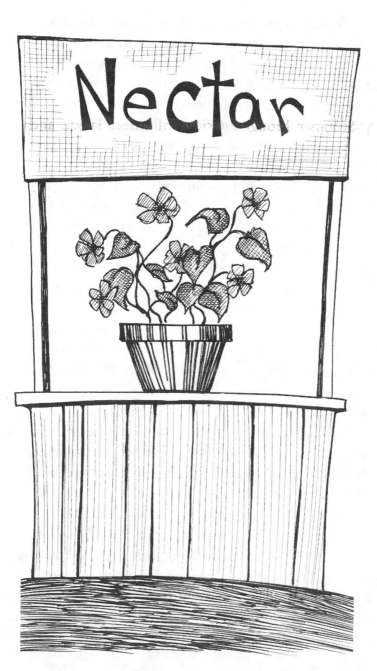

Dark lines on the lowest petal point to the center of the flower. Insects will land on this petal and follow the dark lines to the flower center. This petal, by its position, color, and stripes, advertises the presence of nectar. The back of the lowest petal is a small tube. Within the tube, or spur, the violet stores its nectar.

A small bee flies to the flower. It has spotted the violet because the flower is blue. (Bees can see blue better than they can see some other colors.) The bee lands on the lowest petal and follows the lines to the center of the violet. As it sips the nectar, the bee rubs against a fuzzy yellow "mustache" near the center of the violet and collects pollen on its body. It will carry this pollen to another violet to help that plant make seeds.

Another bee will land on this violet and drop pollen from another plant. Then this violet will be able to make seeds.

The violets bloom early; not many insects are out yet. Perhaps this plant won't receive pollen from another violet. Still, the plant could make seeds by itself. It has been created to do so. You see, after the violet has blossomed, it continues to make leaves. Under these leaves it makes new flowers. Not many people or insects notice these second flowers. They have tiny petals, grow under the leaves, and do not open. They look like tiny buds that have not developed. Yet they do develop, although they remain closed. These pale flowers make seeds without the help of insects. So if the spring has been cold and insects have not been out, the violet plant will still produce its seed.

When the seeds are ripe the pods surrounding them split open into three parts. Each part looks like a tiny canoe filled with seeds. As the "canoes" dry and shrink, the seeds pop out. Some seeds can land almost ten feet away from the "canoe."

Some seeds will be eaten by birds, others will be attacked by insects, others will land where they cannot grow. But some seeds may develop, and in four or five years another violet plant may blossom.

The new violet may have difficulties to face — heat, mold, other plants, animals, and insects. Yet it may grow. Its blossoms will be perfectly formed to attract early insects and to release pollen on those insects. To guarantee seeds, the violet will also make its second small flowers automatically.

A violet blooms in the woods, tribute to a Creator's care. If he so clothes the flowers of the field, how much more shall he clothe you, O ye of little faith?

My Passion Plant

I didn't think much of the plant when I got it. It was a "gift" for joining a plant-of-the-month club and paying my bill promptly. When it arrived it was a scrawny thing, hardly deserving, I thought, of the term *plant*. One skinny stem and a few yellow-green leaves — that was it, my passion plant. I didn't know why it was named "passionflower." I always had assumed that if something was passionate it showed a lot of emotion. This plant showed no emotion at all; in fact, it looked like it might die without a struggle. It had no flowers and looked like it never would, so I called it my passion plant. Not really expecting anything to happen, I put the plant in a clay pot, watered it according to the directions, and exposed it to as much sunlight as possible.

Nothing much happened to my passion plant for a few months. It didn't grow, but it didn't die either. It just sat in the pot, drinking up any water I'd give it. Then spring came, and suddenly the plant took off. It grew like a weed; it didn't bush out, it just grew straight up. Little tendrils grew out of the stem and wound themselves around anything nearby — they choked the "baby spiders" from the spider plant, they threatened the piggyback plant, and they wound around the plant stand. Every other day the passion plant seemed to cry for more water. If a plant can possibly droop loudly, this plant did. It demanded attention. I'd have to check those wild tendrils to be sure they weren't choking other plants. I'd have to water the plant, and I'd have to spray water on the leaves to keep the plant alive. Finally I had to put it in a bigger pot and give it something to climb on.

By this time I had read a little about passion-flowers. They're so named because their flowers are supposed to remind people of the passion of Christ. (*Passion* in this sense means endurance of great suffering.) Passion plants are climbers; that's why they have tendrils. They usually grow in warm climates like Florida, but some are found as far north as Pennsylvania. Some people eat the fruit of the passion plant; it's supposed to be a large berry with several seeds. Passion plants growing in the wild, according to the books I read, are supposed to flower from June to September.

My passion plant was growing wild, but not in the wild. "June to September" came and went, and my passion plant didn't flower. Finally in December a bud appeared, and I was ecstatic. By this time I was pretty passionate about my passion plant; I was going to see a flower. The bud grew to an absolutely monstrous size; I thought it would fall off the stem. But it refused to open. It was time for us to leave on Christmas vacation, and the bud hadn't opened. I didn't want to leave my passion plant, but I did.

Two weeks later we came back, and the bud was on the floor. I almost apologized to the plant for leaving it at such a critical time. I promised to take extra special care of it if only it would produce one flower.

Four months later — sixteen months after I had received my scrawny little plant — it flowered. I had watched a little bud grow to absolutely enormous proportions again. Finally on a Saturday morning it looked like it was going to open. For three hours I watched, absolutely fascinated, as the bud opened to reveal one of the most beautiful flowers I've ever seen. Finally, I could understand why people have named it the passionflower. It really was a symbol of Jesus' suffering.

Ten petals and sepals — five a creamy white and five a light lavender — circled the inner flower parts. The petals, I read, represent the ten faithful disciples. Judas had betrayed Jesus and Peter had denied him. A purple fringe on the inside of the petals represented the crown of thorns that Jesus had worn. Five anthers — the parts that contain the pollen — represented the wounds that Jesus received, two in his hands, two in his feet, and one in his side. Three stigmas — the parts that receive the pollen — represented three nails that held him to the cross. The deeply parted leaves of the plant resembled Roman spears, and the tendrils from the stem looked like little whips with which Jesus was scourged. It was a beautiful symbol. Ten hours after it opened, it closed and fell off the stem.

It's been a year since the flower closed and fell. I've transferred the plant to a bigger pot. I water it faithfully. I spray the leaves about four times a week. I keep it out of drafts and in the sun. I baby that plant as if it were an only child. It hasn't bloomed again.

This year, when we celebrate Jesus' death and resurrection, I would love to have my passion plant flower. It would give me a beautiful symbol of a beautiful event. Maybe my plant is more symbolic than I thought. Maybe it will bloom only once.

Goldenrod, a Weed?

If it's late summer or early autumn, you can be sure that goldenrod is out! All over North America it pokes its head up in fields, blooms along highways, and claims any little piece of ground it can find.

If you're not certain what goldenrod looks like, just go outside during the right season. There will probably be some growing near you. The plants can grow knee-high or can reach well over your head. Each plant sports a yellow flower plume. The "flowers" look almost like soft yellow brushes.

Actually, those "soft yellow brushes" aren't individual flowers. Take time to look at goldenrod and you'll see that each brush is made of hundreds of tiny yellow flowers. If you can take more time, look more closely. You may need a magnifying glass for this. Look at one of the tiny flowers and you'll see that it is actually made up of still tinier flowers. There are strap-shaped flowers around the edges and round flowers in the middle. Imagine how many millions of tiny goldenrod flowers bloom in one field!

Some people don't even like to think about that. They say that they're allergic to goldenrod. It gives them hay fever, they claim.

It's true that at the time of year when goldenrod blooms many people walk around sniffing, sneezing, and wheezing. They're allergic to something. But that something usually isn't goldenrod.

You see, all that sniffing, sneezing, and wheezing usually comes from pollen in the air. Pollen is that yellow "dust" that flowers produce to help make their seeds. If you breathe in pollen or get it in your eyes or mouth, your body may react with drippy eyes or a tickling nose, or worse.

But goldenrod pollen doesn't float in the air. It's heavy and sticky — created to cling to the legs and backs of insects that visit the flower. So the sneezers and wheezers aren't sneezing and wheezing from goldenrod pollen — unless they've been visited by several insects recently.

There are other flowers out at the same time, ragweed especially. Its flowers are green, so people don't notice them very often. But ragweed pollen gets in the air. It's light and it floats — even into noses and mouths. That's usually what people react to.

Most people call goldenrod a weed. I don't agree with most people. A weed generally is a plant that grows where it's not wanted. I think that God wants goldenrod to grow exactly where he put it. So we can't call it a weed. That may sound bold, but let me explain.

Many flowers have finished blooming by late summer. They've dried up and are making seeds. Goldenrod continues to bloom after other flowers have died. Many insects feed on flower pollen. So goldenrod is their main source of food for a while. In fact, it may be their only source in autumn.

More than one thousand different kinds of butterflies, moths, beetles, flies, and bees feed on goldenrod. At night several of these same insects hide in the flower heads. Nights become cooler, but the flowers will give these insects some warmth. A goldenrod flower is much warmer at night than a dried leaf or a bare seed.

Also, during the days, wasps, some flies, spiders, and brownish ambush bugs visit goldenrod. These creatures prey on other insects. At this time of the year they too seem to know where their food will be.

In fact, these creatures have been created to blend with goldenrod flowers. Many of the spiders you'll find there are colored yellow, just like the flowers. Ambush bugs have brown, angular bodies which look like small bits of dead leaves that have fallen on the plants. Syrphid flies are often yellow, black, and hairy. They look just like bees, so other insects "think" that they have come for pollen.

How can we say that goldenrod isn't wanted when some creatures have been created to blend with its flowers?

Even the goldenrod stem doesn't stand unused.

Tiny red aphids (plant lice) cling to the stem, sucking the plant juices. Some flies and moths lay their eggs within the safety of the stem.

Inside the stem a gallfly larva works a little miracle. Early in the summer a female gallfly lays eggs, one inside of each young goldenrod stem. During late summer, a wormlike larva hatches from each egg and produces a tiny bit of a substance. This substance "tells" the plant to swell into a lump around the larva. The larva grows in this lump on the stem. Throughout the winter, after the goldenrod has died, the lump remains on the stem and the larva is safe inside. In the spring the larva chews its way to the hard outer shell of the dead stem. Then it will stop and, in a miracle of change, become an adult gallfly.

God has given this adult fly the perfect tool for pushing its way out of the stem's hard outer shell. Inside the front of its head is a tiny bubble. As the fly pushes its head against the stem, that bubble beats in and out like a tiny jackhammer. The stem's outer shell breaks and the fly crawls out.

Another insect — a moth — also uses the goldenrod stem. A female lays her eggs in the stem in autumn. All winter the eggs are well protected within the stem. They hatch in the spring, and each larva chews its way through the stem to the outside. Then it plugs the hole with silk and stays inside the stem. Again a miracle of change takes place: an adult moth is formed within the stem. This moth simply pushes out the silken plug, crawls out of the stem, dries its wings, and flies away.

The goldenrod is home to that moth and the gallfly. It's a warm shelter for many creatures and a restaurant for thousands of insects. If they could think, they certainly wouldn't call goldenrod a weed. It's right where they need it. Of course it is — God put it there when he created all the creatures that use it. How can we possibly call goldenrod a weed?

A Plant Especially for Kids

I think that God made this plant especially for kids. He certainly designed it so that it would grow just right. Of course, he designed all plants so that they would grow just right, but he gave this one something a little special.

You can't see anything special about the seed. It's just a little grain, but all seeds are like that when you look at them closely. The very middle of the seed has a little part that will grow into a plant and a little part that will grow into roots. It's got lots of food inside the seed to feed the little shoots. Wrapped around the future shoots and the seed food is a hard, protective cover, to ensure that the seed won't be damaged before it's planted. The seed is designed and protected well, as are most seeds.

The plant that grows from the seed is also well-designed and well-protected. The root system is not very big, so the plant isn't always anchored well. Extra roots grow from the base of the plant above the ground. They help prop up the plant.

Most plants related to this one have hollow stems, but this plant's stems are filled with soft, spongy tissue. The tissue is rich in sugars and starches, so it makes good food for animals.

Joints, or nodes, separate sections of the stem. Because they're tough and hard, they strengthen the stem. Because the nodes are placed closer together near the bottom of the plant, that part is stronger. The top of the plant is more flexible and sways easily in the breeze. This plant hardly ever snaps apart in a strong wind.

Long leaves clasp the stem tightly and help strengthen it. The veins in the leaves run lengthwise, making the leaf flexible. A strong central rib makes the leaf tough, and wavy edges prevent tearing. The leaf is well-designed. It won't break apart easily. It will remain on the plant to make food for the plant.

So far the plant is just a plant, designed to do its work. Yet when it's growing, there's one characteristic which might tell you that it's for kids. Most plants in this family grow seven to ten feet high. Only full-grown people can pick the fruit, and they have to stretch. But this plant grows only four to six feet tall, so kids can pick the fruit if they stretch.

The fruit of this plant is especially for kids. It grows like other fruits of its kind.

The pollen grows on tassels. When the pollen is ripe, little anthers, or pollen bags, hang out of the tassels. The wind shakes the anthers, and about ten

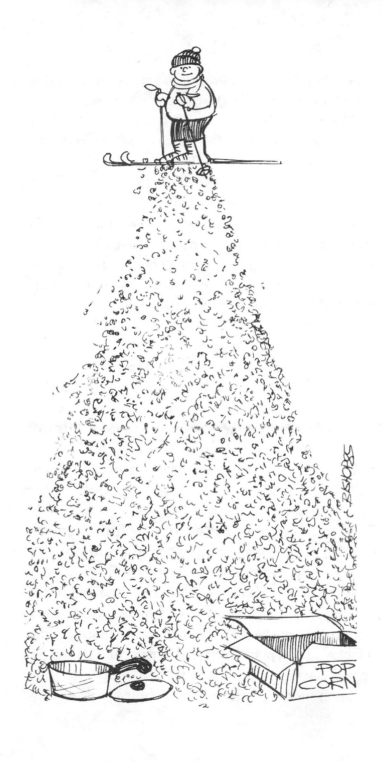

million pollen grains fall out. All those grains blow in the wind to fertilize other plants of its kind.

The part of the plant which will become the fruit is well-protected. Many little ovaries of the fruits-to-be sit like little pearls on a thick central stalk. Leaves are wrapped tightly around the whole stalk to keep insects out and protect it from the weather.

Because the little ovaries are wrapped up so tightly, they must have a special way to collect the pollen. Pollen would do no good resting on the protective leaves. So each ovary has a tiny, silky thread which grows from it and reaches out beyond the protective leaves. Each silky thread is covered with fine hairs to catch pollen.

As each grain of pollen lands on the hairs, it grows a tube through the thread to the protected ovary. Within each ovary is an ovule, or a seed-to-be. When the pollen reaches the ovule, a seed is formed. The ovary around it begins to grow and forms a fruit. Hundreds of tiny fruits grow on each protected stalk. The fruits become big and juicy within their protective leaves.

At this stage, adults often pick the fruits from the big plant and eat them, but they're not ready for kids yet. God has a little work to do on them.

If the fruits stay on the plant until the end of the growing season they become very hard and dry. Each little fruit looks like the seed that was first planted. In fact, you can plant each dried fruit for a new crop. Or you can take the stalks of dried fruit inside and dry them more. When they're completely dried they look like hard little kernels; but packed inside each one is a surprise, especially for kids.

Put the hard little kernels in a pan and heat them. When they reach a certain temperature the moisture inside of them changes to steam. The steam can't escape because the kernels have such hard covers. Finally the pressure inside becomes too great, and the kernel explodes — into popcorn!

That well-protected kid-sized plant was made to produce popcorn. You can grow it yourself from popcorn kernels, if you want to. That's what the kernels are for — either growing or eating. It's fun both ways. Now don't you think that God made the popcorn plant especially for kids?

Mr. Munson's Sparkle Dust

M r. Munson worked with my dad. That didn't impress me, a little kid of four-going-on-five. But because he worked with Dad he'd sometimes come to our house for supper. That did impress me because he always took his foam rubber rabbits and his wonderful sparkle dust.

He made a little game of it. He'd shake hands with everyone and then sit down on the couch, pretending not to notice me at all. I'd have to wait until I thought I would pop. Finally, I'd tug on his sleeve and whisper, "Did you bring your rabbits?"

"My rabbits," he'd puzzle. "Did I bring my rabbits?" And he'd dig a hand deep inside a pocket. "I don't know. Let me see . . . oh yes, here's one."

His hand would slide up slowly, balled into a great big fist. He'd turn it over, open his fist, and out would pop a little foam rubber rabbit.

"Do your trick. Do your trick." I'd dance around him.

"Well, first I need some sparkle dust." He'd put the trick off as long as he could, slowly closing his fingers around the rabbit. Then he'd search through all his pockets until he came up with a tiny envelope. He'd always pretend that he couldn't find it, but I *knew* he wouldn't forget the sparkle dust.

Then he'd shake a tiny bit of the sparkle dust into his free hand and let me look at it for just a minute. I never let on that I couldn't see it sparkle, that it looked like plain dust or dirt to me. After all, it *was* sparkle dust.

He would rub the wonderful sparkle dust all over the fist that held the rabbit, say a few words, and open that hand. Out would pop four or five tiny foam rubber rabbits!

I never could figure out how he did that. When he had only one rabbit, I'd try to peek underneath it. But it always looked like it lay flat on his hand. But then later there would be four or five! He claimed it was the sparkle dust.

He never had much sparkle dust with him. He said his supply at home was running low. Somehow he always ran out of sparkle dust just before it was time to eat.

I haven't seen Mr. Munson for years. I've always wondered if he ever completely exhausted his supply of sparkle dust. If he has, I'd like to tell him that I have a new supply for him.

My sparkle dust doesn't sparkle either. Maybe I just can't see it sparkle. After all, I never really saw Mr. Munson's dust sparkle.

But my dust has something far better than a sparkle. It's made in beautiful little designs, thousands of designs.

Anyone looking at my sparkle dust would think it's just greenish-yellow dust. Anyone with normal eyes, that is. You need very special microscope-eyes to see the designs. I don't have microscope-eyes, so I just use a regular microscope.

When I put my sparkle dust under a microscope, it appears to change. Suddenly it seems to break apart, from just a whisper of dust to hundreds of little pieces. Some pieces are shaped like little sunbursts, others look like tiny fortune cookies. I can see miniature helmets and canoes and barbells and crystals. When I look at my sparkle dust with my own eyes again, I see only dust. But I know that those wonderful shapes are there.

I think that Mr. Munson would love to see my sparkle dust. Wouldn't he be surprised to find out that I have discovered not merely one but thousands of kinds of sparkle dust? Each of those shapes belongs to a different kind of dust. Sometimes I can scoop up several shapes in one handful — mixed sparkle dust. If I try really hard, I can get one pure kind of dust — all miniature sunbursts, all miniature canoes, or the like.

I would try really hard to get a pure sparkle dust for Mr. Munson. You see, mixed dust doesn't work too well on only one thing. You need a certain type of sparkle dust for each object. He couldn't use mixed sparkle dust on his foam rubber rabbit to get more tiny rabbits.

I wouldn't quite know how to tell him this, but

I think my sparkle dust is far more wonderful than his was. Could I convince him that my dust is alive?

Honest and truly, it is! Each miniature sunburst, fortune cookie, helmet, canoe, and so on is really a tiny one-celled speck of life. Each barbell can actually help make thousands of other barbells, and each starburst makes hundreds of starbursts. Not only can they do that, but each live speck of sparkle dust helps to make another whole sparkle dust factory! And that factory is alive, too!

You see, my sparkle dust works on flowers. It really does! And it works because it's alive.

What kind of flower do you like? Sunflowers? There is such a thing as sunflower sparkle dust. That's the sunburst kind.

One little sunburst speck of sunflower sparkle dust lands on a sunflower. We can't even see the sunburst unless we have those microscope-eyes. But it's there, and somehow it knows it's there, because it's alive.

Immediately after landing, this sunburst begins "searching" for a certain part of the sunflower, the part that can make a seed. Suddenly, the sunburst grows a little tube — little to us, but very long for the tiny sunburst. This "little" tube can grow hundreds of times longer than the sunburst itself.

Finally the sunburst tube reaches the part of the sunflower that can make a seed. That speck of life in the sunburst travels down the tube and joins another speck of life in the seed part. They grow together and actually make a sunflower seed.

Mr. Munson could plant that sunflower seed, raise a sunflower plant, and he'd have his very own sunburst sparkle dust. You see, the sunflower is a sunburst sparkle dust factory. Mr. Munson would never have to look for sparkle dust again — at least not for sunflower sparkle dust.

That's another good thing about my sparkle dust; it's absolutely free. At certain times of the year, especially in the spring, there's an unlimited supply. It floats in the air, it dusts bicycle seats, and it blows against screens.

Some people think that it's just greenish-yellow dust, but I know that it's really sparkle dust. I know that it is alive, that it has beautiful shapes, and that each shape works on a different plant to make seeds and more plants and more sparkle dust. Some people call it pollen, but I like to call it sparkle dust.

I would love to find Mr. Munson and tell him about pollen — that wonderful, living sparkle dust of unlimited supply. Of course he would have to change his trick. He'd have to use a flower instead of a foam rubber rabbit, and the trick would take a little longer. But it would be far more wonderful, because it makes more living flowers, not just four or five foam rubber rabbits. And he would never run out of sparkle dust just before it's time to eat.

But then, even when I was four-going-on-five, I had a little doubt about Mr. Munson's limited supply of sparkle dust. I never told him, but once I peeked out of the front window when he came up our walk. Just before he reached the porch, he took that tiny envelope out of his pocket. He reached down, picked up a little dirt, and put it into the envelope. He rang the bell only after he had the envelope safely tucked back into his pocket. Ever since then, I've had a suspicion that Mr. Munson's "limited" supply of sparkle dust was really just plain dirt.

Come to think of it, some people think that my sparkle dust is "just plain pollen." Maybe Mr. Munson's dust was just as wonderful as mine.

And I must admit, there's one thing that still has me puzzled. I never did figure out that foam rubber rabbit trick.

A Very Special Plant

It's a very special plant. Its flowers grow in clusters, and there are several clusters on each plant. Each cluster has over fifty tiny flowers, so there are well over one hundred flowers on each plant.

As each flower opens, its petals fold back so that they are hardly noticeable. When you glance at the flower, you think you're looking at five petals, but you're not. You're really looking at special nectar cups which hold the sweet juice of the flower. Each nectar cup has a little horn which curves in toward the center of the flower. Each flower smells very sweet, and the nectar is delicious to insects.

Other flowers often have a ring of stamens. The stamens have little bags of pollen on top of a small stalk. If you touch the stamens, your finger will look like it has a yellow (or brown or purple) dust on it. That's the pollen.

The pistils in the center of the ring of stamens are important because they contain ovules, or seeds-to-be. The ovules become seeds only if pollen is dusted on them.

Pollen is carried from the stamens to the pistil or pistils of other flowers by insects or birds or by the wind. The stamens of most flowers are right out in the open so that the pollen can be easily picked up and carried to a pistil.

But this plant is different. The pollen is hidden deep inside the middle of each flower, where it seems no insect, bird, or breeze can touch it. If you look at the flower closely, you will see that the five nectar cups surround a roundish, fat, little fleshy stump. The stump is completely closed except for five tiny slits, which you can see between the nectar cups. Inside this stump grow five stamens with their pollen, and the pistil. It seems that it would be almost impossible for the pollen inside that "stump" to ever reach the pistil of another flower to make seeds. Yet every year it happens, more times than we can count. Here's how.

Attracted by the sweet nectar in the cups, an insect will visit the flower. Because the flower is so tiny and its parts are so smooth, the insect has trouble. Its feet slip, and the flower bends under its weight. The only way it can keep from slipping off the flower is to put its feet into the slits between the nectar cups.

On the top of each slit is a tiny black clip. When the insect puts its legs into the slit, its feet are wedged into the clip. When the insect has drunk the nectar and is ready to move to another flower, it pulls its legs out of the slits. Out of each slit come the tiny black clips attached to the insect's feet. Two bags of pollen hang from each clip.

Many flowers have powdery pollen which "dusts" insects or blows easily in the wind. But the pollen of this plant is waxy and sticks together in little clumps. As the insect flies to another flower, the waxy pollen hangs on, clipped to the insect's legs.

The insect goes to another flower and slips its feet into another slit. This time the pollen bags break off and are left in the slit.

At the back of each slit there's a sugary liquid. The pollen grains can grow in this liquid. They push out little tubes that grow into the pistil to the ovules, the seeds-to-be. Once the pollen reaches the ovules, seeds are formed. As the nectar cups fall away and the seeds begin to grow, the stump swells and becomes a seed pod.

Like the flowers, the seeds of this plant are also very special. They depend on the wind, rather than on insects or animals, to be scattered. As the seeds grow within the pod, each seed develops silky white hairs. When the seeds are ready, the pod splits open and tufts of white "silk" spread out. A breeze lifts this "silk" and its attached seed out of the pod and carries it far from the plant. If the seed hits a tree or a stone or a fence, it separates from its silky parachute and falls to the ground. Next spring a new plant may grow where the seed has landed.

This special plant, created so perfectly for its seed making and seed spreading, is also very special to certain insects. The stems and leaves of this plant contain a milky juice. Many birds don't like the taste of this juice at all; they become sick if they eat it. But a certain caterpillar loves the taste of these leaves and spends most of its time eating them. When the caterpillar becomes a bright orange butterfly, it contains the taste of this plant within its body. Birds "know" that they don't like the flavor of this butterfly; it tastes too much like the plant. So they never try to catch this butterfly. The butterfly is protected by the juice of this plant.

In fact, some birds won't eat any orange butterflies that look at all like the butterfly which has eaten this plant. Some orange butterflies which have never seen this plant are protected by it.

It's a very special plant in many ways, and yet it's a very common plant. It's the milkweed. Most of us have seen its seed pods split open in fields or along roadsides every autumn. Most of us just didn't realize that it is such a special plant. But then, isn't every plant, in its own way, a very special plant?

Pitcher Plants

M ost insects feed on plants. They eat the seeds, chew the roots, pierce the stems, chomp the leaves, or draw nectar from the flowers. Some insects do several of these things. Most of the time the plants don't mind — if plants could mind — because they are often pollinated in return. Often a plant depends on an insect to help it make seeds. I suppose that it "figures" it can pay for the service with a bit of nectar or a piece of leaf.

However, some plants have "turned the tables," almost as if they are punishing insects for all the bites and chomps the bugs have taken. These plants actually eat insects! To add insult to injury, they don't simply reach out and grab a bug; they lure the poor unsuspecting creature into them. If I were a bug, I would almost be embarrassed to admit that I had been lured into one of these plants. But usually bugs don't live to tell the tale.

Pitcher plants are just what they sound like —

little pitchers of liquid. The leaves have been rolled about and sealed so that each leaf, instead of lying flat like most self-respecting leaves would, is a greedy little pitcher.

Pitchers of plain water don't usually attract many insects; pitchers of sweet lemonade or Kool-aid do. So the pitcher plant has added sugar — really a nectar — to attract the bugs. Instead of mixing the nectar with the water at the bottom of the pitcher, this plant drips it down the outside of its container.

An unsuspecting ant walks up the outside of the pitcher plant, slurping the nectar all the way. When it reaches the top of the pitcher it goes right over the rim to the inside, because there's a zone of sweet nectar along the inside rim. It's almost like free candy.

As soon as it's inside the plant the ant is trapped, for all practical purposes. It simply doesn't know its situation. After it has slurped up sweetness from the nectar zone, the greedy little unsuspecting insect searches for its "candy" farther in the pitcher. As it walks down the inside surface it begins to sense that something is wrong. It's not walking anymore, it's sliding down a very slippery wall toward a pool of water. The pitcher plant, of course, has been made very slippery on the inside so that even ants, which can walk upside down on ceilings with no problem, slide helplessly down.

Suddenly the ant's feet catch on something just a fraction of an inch above the pool. The glassy side of the pitcher has become rough with stiff hairs. Desperately the ant struggles to catch a foothold on

the hairs, but each hair points downward toward the pool. For each step up, the ant falls two steps closer to the pool.

The hairs in the pitcher plant are very special. They signal this disguised leaf that an insect is struggling within it. Digestive juices begin to flow from the plant. The inside of the "pitcher" becomes more slippery, the ant struggles harder, and more digestive juices flow. The ant is fighting a losing battle. Slowly but surely it drops into the pool and drowns.

The water at the bottom of the pitcher contains digestive juices. The wall of the pitcher plant slowly absorbs the useful substances from the drowned ant. The greedy little insect has become the victim of a greedy little plant. The eater has become the eaten. Someone from the ant's colony should have told it not to accept "candy" from strange plants.

Sometimes flies and beetles are attracted to the pitcher plant by its shape and color. They are usually also doomed when they set foot inside the pitcher. Even if they try to fly out they are trapped, since the pitcher often has a "lid" loosely attached to the top. Flying insects bump the lid and fall into the pool. The pitcher plant has "thought" of everything.

This deceptive little plant isn't always a winner, however. Sometimes birds will slit the pitcher with their sharp beaks. Water and insect skeletons pour out. The pitcher is doomed, but the bird has a ready-made meal of dead insects.

A certain spider sometimes spins a web over the top of the pitcher. The spider looks so much like the plant that hungry insects don't notice it. Instead of reaching the sweet nectar zone, the insects tumble into the spider's web. The pitcher below remains empty. The little spider has outwitted both the pitcher plant and the insects.

Once in a while a certain type of fly or mosquito will lay eggs in the water at the bottom of the pitcher plant. The larva that hatch feed on the skeletons of the insects that fell into the pitcher. When the adult fly or mosquito hatches, it simply flies out of the plant. Why it doesn't slip back into the pool or bump the lid, no one knows — not even the pitcher plant.

Of course, the pitcher plant doesn't "know" how to catch insects. It grows in soil that doesn't have much nitrogen, so it was created to obtain its nitrogen from insects. It really doesn't think. Neither does the ant.

If they did think, I'd probably warn the ant and maybe scold the pitcher plant. But then, lots of insects feed on plants, so why can't a plant eat insects? And the pitcher plant feeds birds and some spiders. They all seem to get along just right, without thinking at all for themselves. I guess the Creator thought for all of them when he put them together.

For the Birds

I hate to admit it, but I can't recognize poison ivy. At least I don't think I can. Either that, or I've never seen it or been near it. And that's very unlikely. I think I've probably walked right through it already and simply not recognized it.

I can recognize the greyish-brown dry stem with little rootlets growing from it. I mean the stem you see before the leaves come out. That's the stage poison ivy was at early last spring when our plant taxonomy class looked at it. I never went back to the plants I *knew* were poison ivy when the leaves were out.

I can tell you what poison ivy looks like; I suppose almost anyone can. The plant climbs like a vine or grows like a bush. The greenish-white flowers grow in clusters. The developing berries change from pale green to grayish white. The leaves can be shiny or dull, with notched or smooth edges. The best clue to poison ivy is the presence of three leaflets in each leaf. Very rarely a leaf may have five leaflets.

I *thought* I could tell you what poison ivy looks like. But after rereading the description I just gave, I realize that no one can do a really good job of it. Descriptions are always loaded with *or*s — "smooth or toothed," "shiny or dull," "vine or bush." I guess that the plant just doesn't stand up and shout, "POISON IVY!"

Most people I know claim that they can spot poison ivy instantly. They usually have harrowing stories to tell of sorry encounters with the plant. Now the sight of those three (sometimes five) leaflets is forever imprinted in their minds.

I guess that's why I'm ashamed to admit my ignorance. Usually such an admission is greeted with "You *really* can't spot poison ivy? Tsk, tsk," as if it were a flaw in my character.

I'm happy to report that I'm not the only person alive with that character flaw. A recent book about poisonous plants reported that many people will tell you exactly what *Rhus radicans* (the scientific name) looks like, while they're standing in the middle of a large poison-ivy patch.

I have no harrowing tale to tell of the time *I* itched for days or swelled up miserably from poison ivy. I never did. Someone once told me that seven out of every ten people are allergic to poison ivy. I must be one of the three nonallergics.

That can change at any time, I'm told. Anyone can suddenly develop an allergy to anything at any age. Enjoy your non-allergies while you have them. They might disappear.

Poison ivy really isn't poison, you know. Poisons work on your systems from within to poison you. Poison ivy works from outside to give you a red, itchy rash, perhaps swelling and blisters. Your skin reacts to something it's allergic to. I suppose poison ivy should really be called "allergic ivy."

You can react to almost any part of the plant. The reaction is caused by a mixture of chemicals, called catechols, in the sap. The sap, of course, is found in all parts of the plant. It's oily and will stick to anything — clothes, tools, and animal fur. You could, in a roundabout way, get poison ivy from your cat.

Lest you think that poison ivy is all bad, let me introduce you to its good points. Birds eat the berries. The sap can be made into an inky-black stain, usable only by non-allergics.

Also, poison ivy is in the cashew family, so it has some very well-known, delicious relatives. Cashew nuts are those little lima-bean-shaped nuts that most people pick first from a bowl of mixed nuts. Delicious, and not poison at all. However, you rarely see them in the shells, because said shells contain a poison very much like poison ivy. The oil from cashew shells is sometimes used to make electrical insulation for airplanes. Why, I don't know. Understandably, some people are allergic to electrical insulation found on airplanes.

Poison ivy is a very close relative of our non-poisonous sumac trees. Sumac wood can be used to make a bright yellow dye. Sumac bark has been used in tanning leather. North American Indians used

to make a beverage from the red staghorn sumac berries.

Poison ivy is related to the Japanese lacquer tree whose sap is also poisonous when it's wet. As that sap dries, it hardens to form a smooth, black, enamel-like substance. Japanese often use that sap to decorate bowls and boxes, thus making Oriental lacquerware.

Poison ivy is also related to the mango tree. If you've ever lived in tropical regions or you have a good grocery store, you know how delicious mangoes are. Sometimes a mango fruit stem will cause an allergic reaction. (You usually don't eat the stems, so you don't have to worry.)

Last, but not least, poison ivy is related to the pistachio tree. Pistachios are those little nuts that you can buy, still in the shell, dyed red. I never did find out why people dye them red. They grow brown, like most nuts, and they're delicious just as they come off the tree. Pistachio shells are not poisonous. They don't cause any allergies either.

As you can see, most of poison ivy's good points belong to its relatives, not to the poison ivy plant at all. It shouldn't really stand on (or creep over) its cousin's tastiness or a distant relative's lack of poison.

What redeeming features does poison ivy itself have? Birds eat the berries, but poison ivy has nothing to recommend it to *you*.

I've been mulling this over for several days lately. My train of thought was launched when my father-in-law asked me if I had seen poison ivy in our woods. I sheepishly admitted that I couldn't identify the stuff, hung my head in shame, and found myself looking at three leaflets.

Soon I began searching for a list of poison ivy's good points — something to comfort myself with if I began to itch. I never itched and I never found many good points. I did begin to wonder.

Why do you suppose God would make a plant that caused so much misery and did so little good? Why couldn't he just have created the cashew, pistachio, mango, and lacquer trees and dispensed with the poison ivy? After all, only a few birds eat the berries.

That's it! Birds eat the berries. God put us in charge of creation, but he didn't create everything in the world only for our pleasure. He created for his pleasure. Poison ivy doesn't really give many of us pleasure, but we can stay away from it. Certain birds seem to like it. Maybe it pleased God to make a plant just for its own sake and for the birds.

Dead of Winter

The month of January is the "dead of winter" in North America. Of course, winter doesn't hit our southern states very hard. People who live in Florida, Texas, southern California, or similar areas are, in my opinion, particularly blessed. They may see green plants, live bugs, and real sunshine the year round. But those of us who live in northern states or in Canada know what the dead of winter is all about.

In some areas it's more "dead" than "winter." Maybe we should say that it's really just dormant. Little animals have gone into hibernation, insects have laid their eggs or spun their cocoons, and most plants have turned brown. Maybe there's no howling blizzard outside, but you still know that it's winter.

In my area there's bound to be a howling blizzard some time in January. During this month snow covers the fields, and almost everything outside seems to be merely waiting out the winter. For a nature lover this is not the loveliest time of the year.

Yet I just stumbled into an interesting pastime that could while away the winter months in a hurry. It's walking through a woods or field or along a roadside and trying to identify those brown dead things poking up out of the ground. I know that probably sounds dull to you, but don't stop reading now. You may be surprised.

Take Queen Anne's lace, for example. It grows along almost any highway in the summer. The tiny white flowers are bunched together in an upside-down-umbrella-shaped cluster.

In January you can still find the dried stalks sticking up two or three feet into the air. It looks as if it has a dried Queen Anne's lace cluster on top. All the tiny "flowers" look a little scraggly because they're really fruits now. But they still have the shape you recognize. Sometimes the little "flowers" turn back into the bunch to form a little nest. Look for it, you'll recognize it.

Queen Anne's lace is closely related to the carrot. Its leaves look rather like carrot tops. If you clear the area around the dried plants, you may even be able to find some green, lacy, fuzzy leaves out, and you'll find a yellowy white root that smells suspiciously like carrots.

Try milkweed. It grows in old fields and waste places. You probably know it better by its seedpod than by its flowers anyway. Some of those seedpods are still on the plants in January. They're fat at the bottom, pointed at the top, and packed with silky, tufted seeds. They're the pods that split open down

the middle and then look like little boats filled with frayed silk threads.

Milkweed flowers are tiny but grow in big bunches, just like Queen Anne's lace. For some reason, only one flower in each bunch develops into a seedpod. If you look closely at your dry stalk, you can probably see where the other little flowers were attached.

Try to remember where you found the milkweed, and go back there next summer. The leaves, the flower buds, and the seedpods are supposed to be good to eat — after you boil them to get rid of the bitter milk juice!

Who doesn't recognize a cattail? It grows in marshy areas and looks like a big cigar on a stalk taller than you are. You can still find some cattails in January, although the leaves may be brown and dry. Some "cigars" may look fuzzy or may have disappeared, but usually a few good ones remain.

Those "cigars" are really countless rust-colored flowers packed tightly together. When the tiny flowers become tiny fruits, the spike "explodes." Hairs fluff out and carry the fruits away. Fuzzy cattails have "exploded" only part way. If you pick a cattail and bring it inside, you should put some kind of lacquer on it. Otherwise it may "explode," and you'll have a mess to clean up.

Chicory is a little harder to recognize in the winter. During the summer you've probably noticed some "bushes" with scraggly green branches, a few skinny leaves, and many beautiful blue, daisylike flowers. It usually grows knee-to-waist high along roadsides. The knee-to-waist-high branches remain throughout the winter.

Little knobs poke up where the flowers used to be. If you look closely at the knobs, you can see tiny pieces of dried flower bracts hugging the branches closely. You can't really see much of a stem; the flowers seem to have grown right out of the branch.

Chicory plants have very large taproots. These are often roasted, ground up, and added to coffee. That's usually done from chicory grown for that purpose. But you could try it with your roadside stalks. Who knows? It might work.

You probably know what goldenrod looks like in the fall. Often whole fields and roadsides are bright yellow with this flower. Usually it grows knee- to waist-high with soft-looking plumes of tiny yellow flowers.

You can find goldenrod throughout the winter because bits of the dried flowers stick to the stalks. From a distance they still look plumelike. But the color has become greyish-tan instead of bright yellow.

Take another easy-to-recognize flower. You may not know what this one is called, but you've probably seen it along some highways. It's called mullein, and it grows very tall — over six feet — and it has a spike of yellowish flowers tightly packed together. Each little fruit looks sort of like a turtle's head.

During its first year of growth, mullein produces only a bunch of light green, flannel-like leaves close to the ground. The flower stalk grows the second year. If you look around a dried mullein stalk you may be able to find a first-year rosette of leaves. They often stay green during the winter.

I could go on and on. Think of how many dried sticks, stalks, and bits of flowers dot the fields and roadsides throughout the winter. Each of those was a plant, and each holds some interesting tidbit, even now.

Winter never lasts forever. We have the promise that season will follow season. But during the winter, go out and look around. If you dig a little, you'll find living proof of that promise — little bits of green beneath dried stalks, even in the dead of winter.

Flowers Everywhere

When the weather warms up, spring is on its way. You know that brown grass will turn green, leaf buds will swell, and flowers will pop open. You'll see crocuses, violets, buttercups, maples, and oaks.

Wait a minute! Maples and oaks? Maples and oaks don't have flowers. Or do they? Of course they do. All trees have flowers, and a lot of them are out in early spring.

Let me explain.

You know that maple trees make seeds. They're those little "helicopters," two little wings with the seeds connected in the middle. Sometimes you see them, green, in early summer. Or they may twirl from the tree, brown, in the fall. You also know that oak trees make seeds. Everyone recognizes acorns. They're oak seeds.

These seeds obviously grow someplace on the trees. That makes sense. They don't come from the leaves; leaves never change into seeds. Then where do they come from? From the flowers — maple seeds from maple flowers, acorns from oak flowers.

Now, before we get to those flowers, let's refresh your memory on how flowers make seeds. You need the part that will become a seed. That's called the pistillate part, or pistillate flower. That's the seed-to-be. You also need the part that makes pollen. That's called the staminate part, or staminate flower. The pollen must be brushed on the pistil to fertilize it so it can grow a seed. Some flowers have both parts in one flower. Some plants have only seeds-to-be in one flower and only pollen in another flower.

Are you with me so far? Stick with me. If you get through this, you can see flowers everywhere.

Most flowers that we notice depend on insects to get their pollen to the seeds-to-be. That's why the flowers are brightly colored — so that insects will notice them as well as we do.

But some flowers don't rely on insects. They depend on the wind to scatter their pollen. They make lots of pollen so that some of it will blow against the pistillate, or seed-to-be, parts. These flowers aren't so noticeable. They don't have to attract attention.

Many trees depend on wind to scatter their pollen. So their flowers aren't that noticeable. But they're there. And they're delicate, fascinating little flowers. Look around in the spring; you'll see them.

Most tree flowers bloom before all the leaves are

out on the tree. That way the pollen hits the flowers, not the leaves. So you can see the flowers just before or while the tree is beginning to leaf out.

Look closely at a maple tree. Does it seem like it's covered with soft brushes? You may see some small leaves, but you also see brushy things growing from the twigs. Those brushy things aren't leaves. They're maple flowers. Usually maple flowers have their pollen parts in one flower and their seeds-to-be in another. Both of these types of flowers are small, so there are many, many flowers clustered together on the tree. Usually the flower clusters hang on long, threadlike stems. Because they're on thin stems, they sway easily in any breeze. That makes pollen shake from one flower to another.

Besides that, the staminate flowers (those with pollen) usually house their pollen on the ends of long, slender stalks. Those flowers don't have much, if anything, in the line of petals, since they don't need to attract insects. So the long pollen stalks are simply wobbly stalks on the ends of thin stems. As they tremble in the breeze, they release pollen.

Those thin pollen stalks on thin stems are what make the tree look brushy in the spring. Look at the tree closely again. You're probably looking at maple flowers. Most maple flowers are greenish or yellowish, and are in bloom just before or while the leaves are coming out. Red maples bloom well before the leaves are out, and their flowers are red — small, but red.

Oaks generally leaf out later than maples, so they

flower later also. Oak pistillate flowers, the seeds-to-be, are usually quite difficult to find. They grow in clusters on short stalks, usually near the bases of developing leaves. You won't ordinarily notice these flowers when you walk past an oak tree. But you can't miss the staminate oak flowers, the pollen producers. Just watch an oak tree next spring. These flowers grow closely together in drooping, hairy bunches. These bunches, called catkins, look like soft, green "tree stuff" all packed together on a droopy stalk. You can see them hanging from any oak tree.

If you can reach a green catkin, pull it off the tree and look closely at it. Dozens of pollen flowers are all tightly packed together on that one four-inch, droopy stalk. If you have a little magnifying glass, check out one of these flowers. It's a little wonder. Although it is super tiny, it looks like a little crown — round with little points decorating the top edges. Inside, on slender stalks, grow the pollen bags. They poke up like little yellow jewels in a fuzzy green crown. They really are delightful flowers.

Oak catkins fall from the tree after they've spread their pollen. Those are the messy-looking brown, dead, long things you find near oak trees in late spring. They may look messy then, but they once were beautiful little flowers.

The flowers I've described are only maple and oak. They're common throughout the country. If you go outside and really look, you can probably find them. I've seen them and I think that they're well worth looking at.

Remember, *all* trees have flowers. You don't have to look for maple or oak. Next spring look at any trees near you. Flowers will bloom everywhere. There is so much beauty in this world that goes unnoticed. We really should open our eyes and look.

The "Spruce" Tree

Last December the artificial tree was up in the shopping mall again. Every Christmas season that big green "tree" goes up. Covered with ornaments, it stands straight and tall, trying to look like a stately spruce. And from a distance this tree may look like one, but anyone who comes close to it can't be fooled.

For one thing, it smells like an artificial tree. When I sit on the bench under it, if I smell anything, I smell plastic. A real spruce tree would have a real, pungent spruce odor. Some people think that the odor of a spruce — especially certain types of spruce — is unpleasant, but a real spruce certainly doesn't smell like plastic.

This "tree" is planted in a square pot that is only three feet wide. A real spruce tree would need a much wider area over which to spread its roots. Spruce roots, although they don't grow deep, grow far out from the tree.

For another thing — this "tree" has absolutely no bugs around it; they can't get into the plastic "trunk." In any real spruce, bark beetles burrow under the bark to feed on smaller insects and juices. Inside this "tree," however, there is probably only a column of air, no sap and resins, no life-giving juices flowing constantly up and down the tree.

If this were a real tree that people had cut down, they would be able to make paper from the wood, chewing gum from the resin, and beer from the sap. But this "tree" is artificial. All we'll ever get from it is chopped-up or melted plastic.

Whoever made this "tree" put only a few cones on it. Some spruce trees are overladen with cones. Even after the cones drop their seeds, the empty husks can remain on the tree for almost twenty years. But this tree's artificial "cones" do nothing but sit there. They can't possibly grow into another spruce tree.

These plastic "needles" have no definite shape. The needles of a true spruce, however, always feel square between your fingers. And the plastic "needles" house no insects. Real spruce needles would supply a good meal for a larch sawfly or some spruce budworms.

The branches of this "tree" carry only ornaments. No living thing is found in or around it. If this were a real spruce you could probably spot a woodpecker on the trunk searching for the insects that live there. Crossbills might hop around the branches, using their especially adapted beaks to pluck the cones apart.

A cottontail rabbit might take shelter beneath the tree, and a mouse might make her nest at its base. Bears, wolves, lynx, and foxes may make their homes nearby to feed on the smaller animals that have taken refuge in the tree. The artificial "tree" has nothing of that. It may look like a spruce, but it lacks one essential ingredient — life.

Someone may fool people with a fine imitation of a spruce tree, but the insects, birds, and animals can't be fooled. Life is missing, and no one can put it there.

I really don't mind this imitation spruce. I suppose it even serves a good purpose in decorating the mall. I'm glad that whoever puts it there doesn't go out and chop down a big live spruce every year. But each time I see that "tree" I think of the big difference between it and a real spruce. People may be able to make beautiful imitations, but they're only artificial. Only God can make a real, living tree.

The Apple Factory

Somewhere near you, an apple factory is hard at work. We don't think of it as a factory because it's not a big building. No trucks rumble in with supplies, no smokestacks belch out gray clouds, and no whistles blow. Nobody even works there; the factory runs all by itself. Yet it keeps producing tasty little snacks year after year. It's that plain old apple tree, probably right out in your backyard.

But it really isn't a "plain old apple tree"; it really is an amazing, efficient factory. Let me show you around.

Right around the month of October your apple factory is probably adding a last bit of sugar to this year's crop. So far the apples have been quite hard, and they have tasted rather tart. Anyone touring the factory before mid-October may have wanted to stop the assembly line to see what went wrong. But nothing has gone wrong; the visitors just came too early, that's all.

The sugars in the apples, until now, were complex sugars called carbohydrates. Now they're breaking down into simple sugars that taste sweeter to us. This breakdown of sugars, the last step in the apple assembly line, helps turn hard, tart apples into soft, sweet-tasting ones. The tree factory works this step best in the clear, crisp days of autumn.

If you look around the factory, you'll notice that the apples stored closest to the windows — those on the outer edges of the tree — are the reddest. That's because they get more sunlight than apples stored in the closets — close to the tree trunk.

This apple factory is far busier than it looks at this time of year. Besides putting the final touches in this year's product, it's also making plans for next year. It's beginning to store supplies so that it will be ready to work next spring.

Look closely at the point where the apple stem is connected to the branch. Nearby you should see a little bud. That's the fruit bud for next year's apple. Everything needed to grow an apple is tightly packed inside. The supplies simply haven't been unpacked yet.

You see, this apple factory usually takes time off in the winter. The machinery needs a rest. But before it closes shop completely, it packs its next-year's supplies into weatherproof "cartons." They won't be damaged when the heat is turned down. Buds on the apple tree have scales wrapped tightly around them to protect them from snow and ice. Deep within the buds lay all the apple-flower parts, just waiting for spring.

When spring warms the apple factory, the machinery turns on once more. Sap begins to flow inside the tree. Then supplies are unpacked; flower buds and their leaves begin to swell open. We know that the factory is working because small green leaves and clusters of apple blossoms dot the tree.

If you'd tour your apple factory in the spring, you'd be amazed at how efficient it is. Nothing is wasted. Every supply is there for a purpose.

First, a little cluster of leaves opens up. These are needed to make food for the tree, especially the buds, from sunlight.

As the leaves spread, little blossom buds appear. Each bud is enclosed by five tiny, green, leaf-like things called sepals. They protect the precious inner package. Soon the sepals push back, and you can see scarlet petals that quickly turn pink or almost white as they grow.

Petals help make the apple flowers noticeable and attractive to bees. Apple flowers also produce a sweet juice called nectar to help attract bees. You'll see later where bees fit into the plans.

At the center of each apple blossom grow the supplies for making apples. Twenty little stalks grow in a ring around the base of the petals. On top of each stalk is a little, two-sectioned bag. These stalks-with-bags are called stamens. The bags hold pollen.

Right in the middle of the stamens grows what we call the pistil. The thick bottom part of the pistil, the ovary, will become the apple. Inside it are ten ovules, or seeds-to-be. The top part of the pistil is divided into five little tubes called styles. Each style has a sticky top called a stigma. This sticky stigma must be brushed with pollen. The pollen will then grow a tube down to the ovary and join the ovules to make apple seeds. The fruit grows around the seeds.

Sounds complicated, doesn't it? But then, I suppose most factories are.

Anyway, this is where the bees come in. They come to suck the nectar and to gather pollen to feed their little bees. By springtime their winter supply of honey is used up, so they're eagerly looking for more food. As they move from flower to flower, their bodies become dusted with pollen. They brush against the sticky tips of the pistils, and some pollen rubs off. When this happens a process called pollination has taken place. The pollen can now grow its tube and start to make apple seeds.

If the pollen is from different varieties of apple blossoms, cross-pollination has taken place. Most apple flowers must be cross-pollinated, so the bees are really important. I suppose that you could say the apple factory does have a few workers — the bees.

The petals have served their purpose of attracting bees. Now they wither and fall off. The rest of the flower parts wither also. Only the ovary grows. At first it looks like a little swollen bit of stem below the withered flower parts. Then it becomes bigger and rounder, like a little green ball with withered flower parts at one end.

Now more leaves appear on the trees. The small

apples need food to keep growing, and it's the apple factory's job to supply that food. The leaves take in carbon dioxide gas from the air. Water and minerals are shipped from the roots through the trunk to the leaves. There everything is combined in sunlight to make sugars for the growing apples and for the tree. About forty leaves are needed to make enough food for one apple to grow.

Sometimes, if there are too many apples on the tree — if the factory is overloaded — some green apples will drop off. It's an automatic safety system to ensure that the apples that stay will be well-fed. By the end of the summer, the apples are almost full size.

While all this work has been going on upstairs in the factory — the part where you see the apples growing — the basement floors have not been idle. The roots also have been working. They must supply food from the soil. So they keep spreading, searching for food. They spread underground as far or even a little farther than the outermost leaves reach above the ground.

Apparently, from basement to top floor, from roots to top branches, the apple factory is working well, the apples are growing bigger and bigger. Finally, during the clear, crisp autumn days, they begin to turn red and sweet.

But that's when we came in, isn't it? Our tour is over. In those clear, crisp autumn days the apple factory is in full swing, and the apples are turning red and sweet. Next October pick an apple and look at it. See the papery little things opposite the stem? They're the sepals that protected the flower parts last spring. The stamens and styles are gone. You're holding a package that's been especially made by the apple factory to hold apple seeds. And what a delicious package it is! Take a bite; apples are good for you.

Have you ever heard of packages that you can eat? Here they are, straight from the apple factory. No mess, no pollution, no work, no waste. What an amazing factory! Too bad people can't make factories like that.

Wild Apple Tree

An apple tree once grew along a country road, far from any village or farmhouse. No person had planted the tree; a bird had dropped a seed at that spot. No person tended the tree. It was wild; its apples were tough and sharp. No person even noticed the tree. But other creatures noticed.

Every spring, just as the apple tree began to bud, ruffed grouse appeared as if from nowhere to feast on the buds. Ruffed grouse eat over four hundred different plant foods, but apple buds are high on their list of favorites. Along with the ruffed grouse came ring-necked pheasants, great prairie chickens, and bobwhites. These birds also like to eat apple buds and sometimes even leaves.

Yet the tree had plenty for all. Although birds nipped the buds, the apple tree still blossomed. Then hundreds of bees visited its white flowers. They came to gather pollen and nectar for their hives. Other insects also swarmed around the blossoming tree, eager to feast on the pollen.

As spring wore into summer, the apple tree unfolded its leaves and began to develop its fruit. Birds nested in the tree and still more creatures came to visit. Deer came silently to the tree and nibbled the leaves. Ruffed grouse returned to check on the leaves. Apple leaves are high in vitamin A, calcium, and carbohydrates, which make them good for deer and grouse.

Mice, porcupines, and rabbits also visited the tree to munch on its bark. The inner bark of an apple tree is high in carbohydrates, which provide energy for these woodland creatures. And yet the tree had plenty for all. As summer cooled into autumn, the small, tough apples grew. As days became shorter and colder, more and more creatures visited the tree for its fruit.

The deer returned to pick the ripe fruit off the lower branches. Bears, led by their powerful sense of smell, traveled for miles to eat the juiciest apples they could find. Red foxes moved in to feast on the fruit — one of their favorite foods. During some parts of the year, one-quarter of the foxes' food comes from the wild apple tree.

Birds also visited the tree. Chickadees, crows, crossbills, finches, bluejays, grackles, thrushes, magpies, orioles, rose-breasted grosbeaks, starlings, titmice, towhees, waxwings, and woodpeckers all loved the seeds of the tree. Over thirty different songbirds are attracted to wild apple trees. The

seeds of this tree contain a very concentrated dose of nutrition.

As the apples ripened and fell to the ground, yet more creatures feasted on the fruit. Coyotes, gray foxes, skunks, fishers, raccoons, and squirrels all visited the apple tree for an easy, delicious, and nutritious meal. Each apple supplies water, fruit sugar, pectins, and acids which aid the animals' digestion.

Even while apples rotted on the ground, they provided food for creatures. Yellowjackets alighted on the fallen fruit, attracted by its fermented juice. Snails came to feast on the rotting fruit. Worms flourished in the soil enriched by rotted apples. And woodcocks gathered beneath the tree to search for juicy worms.

As autumn turned to bitter winter, the wild apple tree continued to provide. Often it held much of its fruit on the tree when other trees were bare. When food was scarce, creatures returned to the wild apple tree. The deer returned — this time to pull frozen apples off its lower branches. The deer didn't starve, because the tree was there. Cottontails returned to chew its nutritious bark. Pheasants, bluejays, and squirrels continued to feed on its small, hard fruits. The wild apple tree provided life through the winter.

Every season, every year, the apple tree supplied food for the creatures that visited it. More creatures than you can count came to the tree for food. More birds than you can count nested in its branches.

As the tree grew old, over a hundred years old, it began to hollow out. Then, even as it began to die, it provided shelter for creatures. Countless families of deer mice were raised in nesting sites at the base of the tree. Shrews also made their home there. A woodchuck dug beneath its roots, and a skunk lived at its base. Raccoons found suitable resting places farther up its hollowed trunk, and a woodpecker carved its home still farther up the trunk. Yet the apple tree was not quite dead. It was old, hollow in places, and dying. But it still provided food every season for a few more years.

Then late one autumn, when the apple tree was one hundred and three years old, a person came to the tree. Many people had passed the tree, but none had stopped. This person stopped and looked. He reached up, picked one of the apples, and bit into it. "Ugh," he said, "That's bitter. This tree isn't good for much." How little did he know.

How little do we all know. How easily we pass judgment.

The Trees Fight Back

Most people think that plants don't do much. They believe that trees, bushes, and herbs sit and soak up the sun, drink a little water, and maybe make some flowers and fruits. That's about it, they think.

Not so! Scientists are just beginning to find out something of what goes on in a plant and between plants. Take the case of the chestnut trees.

A healthy chestnut tree can grow to the height of a ten-story building. Its straight, fast-growing trunk is often so large on a mature tree that two people can hardly circle it with their arms. Its spreading branches afford cool summer shade to animals and people alike, and its nuts taste sweet and delicious. A healthy chestnut tree is truly magnificent.

Our story concerns three types of chestnut trees: the Oriental chestnut, the European chestnut, and the American chestnut. All three trees are slightly different from each other, yet all are chestnut trees.

During the early 1900s the American chestnut grew naturally along the east coast of the U.S. From Maine down to Georgia, from the Atlantic coast to the Appalachian mountains, these magnificent trees covered at least one-quarter of the forest land.

Some trees even grew west of the Appalachians. Pioneers had considered the American chestnut *so* important and *so* beautiful that they transplanted the tree as they moved westward. Long after the pioneers were gone those stately trees thrived.

Americans loved to eat chestnuts. In fact, they ate more nuts than American chestnut trees could produce. By 1900, Americans were importing Oriental chestnuts from Japan.

In 1904, a forester in New York state noticed that some American chestnut trees seemed to be unhealthy. Their leaves were yellow, and an orange fungus grew on their trunks. The chestnut blight had arrived.

The blight was that orange fungus. It probably came in a shipment of chestnuts from Japan. Now, Oriental chestnut trees were still healthy. They were slightly different from the American chestnut trees, and that orange fungus didn't seem to bother them.

But that same orange fungus killed the American trees. Slowly but surely, the orange fungus spread from one American chestnut tree to the next. Carried by wind, birds, and mammals, the blight traveled about ten to fifteen miles each year.

By 1923 the orange fungus had attached itself to eight out of every ten American chestnut trees.

By the early 1950s, eight out of every ten trees were dead. By 1970, most of the natural trees in the east had died. Only some transplanted trees survived in Michigan.

Scientists worked hard through the years to save the trees. They tried to find some way to help the trees fight the orange fungus, but they were helpless. So around 1950 they contacted scientists in Italy for help.

You see, European chestnut trees had also suffered a blight. That orange fungus had reached them too, and many of their trees had died. For a long time scientists in Italy watched helplessly while their trees died.

But somehow the European chestnut trees began to come back. Italians noticed new European chestnut trees growing up healthy. These new trees still had a fungus, but it was white, not orange.

European researchers discovered that their trees were fighting back! When attacked by the orange fungus, a young tree would produce some sort of liquid. That liquid would somehow make the fungus less harmful. The fungus would then become white and simply live on the tree without killing it.

American scientists asked Italian scientists for some of that white fungus. Although the European chestnut differed from the American, they thought perhaps the white fungus could save the American trees, too.

It did help. If someone went to an American chestnut tree which had the orange fungus and put

the white fungus on it, the tree would live. Somehow, the white fungus changed the orange fungus. But no American tree could yet produce the liquid which European chestnut trees had produced. No American tree could make the orange fungus turn white all by itself.

The orange fungus was still spreading. People couldn't keep up with it. They couldn't go to every single American chestnut tree and put white fungus on it. For the next twenty years American chestnut trees continued to die. There were very few trees left, and no one could save them. People almost gave up on the American chestnut tree.

Then in 1976 something strange happened. A woman in Michigan checked her old transplanted chestnut tree. It had the orange fungus, but it also had a white fungus! No one had put the white fungus there. Somehow it had simply grown.

Scientists looked at the white fungus and tested it. It was not exactly like the white fungus they had received from Italy. It was different, but it worked. Somehow, that American chestnut tree had produced its own liquid which turned the orange fungus white. In its own way, that American chestnut tree was fighting back!

Since then, scientists have been checking the remaining American chestnut trees in Michigan. Now there are more healthy trees than trees with the orange fungus. And over one-quarter of the diseased trees are fighting back. They are producing their own liquid which turns the orange fungus white and helps the tree to live. Scientists aren't sure exactly what that liquid is. They're simply glad that, when they couldn't help, the trees fought back.

And some people think that plants don't do much! Here we have three different kinds of chestnut trees. Each kind of tree fights the orange fungus in its own way. Each kind of tree fights back.

But I don't think that the trees are fighting back all by themselves. I think that Someone is helping them.

Closing Up Shop

Every autumn, all over the colder parts of North America, creatures prepare for the cold weather ahead. Birds fly south, squirrels lay in a store of nuts and seeds, and bears and groundhogs eat like there's no tomorrow, to store up fat for their winter sleep. They're all active because they've all been given instincts to prepare for winter as best they can.

What about the trees? Trees don't have instincts. Trees aren't active; they just sit there and drop their leaves, right?

Wrong! Of course God didn't give trees instincts; they don't have brains. But he did create them in a way that they could make special preparations for winter. Trees are much more active than you might imagine. You just can't see the activity. Each autumn, trees which lose their leaves become busy closing up shop for the winter.

Throughout spring and summer, the leaves on those trees act like little factories. They take gases from the air; tree roots provide them with water from the soil; and with the help of sunlight they make these into food for the tree. Little green "machines," called chlorophyll bodies, do all this work in the leaves. (These green "machines" are what makes leaves green.)

During winter, nights become cold enough to freeze water in that leafy machinery. Frozen leaves don't work very well. Besides that, water in the ground also freezes during the winter. The tree needs water, not ice, for fuel. So food production must stop some time in the fall.

During October those trees begin to take their machinery apart. Those chlorophyll bodies simply stop working. Like any unused machinery, they begin to fall apart. They don't rust because they're not metal. Instead they die, because they were living bits of leaves.

That's when you start seeing different colors — yellows, reds, oranges, tans, and golds — in leaves. You see, many of the chemicals which make those colors have been in the leaves all along. But those green machines have been the most obvious feature in the leaves. So the leaves appeared green. When the green breaks apart you can see the other beautiful colors.

To understand this, picture yourself in a busy factory. Huge, noisy machines bolted to the floor are working day and night. What do you see in the factory? The machines, of course. But by late October someone has taken those machines away. He's closing

up shop. What do you see? The empty floor. Maybe it's a beautiful polished wood. Surprise! It was there all along, but you didn't see it when the machines covered it.

In the same way, the green machines disappear from the leaves. Then you can see the "factory floor."

But there's much more to closing up shop than just taking out the machinery. If you want to use the building again later, you should be sure that it doesn't leak. You don't want snow to drift through the windows, and you don't want the pipes to crack. You probably should plug up any cracks and drain some pipes.

That's just what those trees do in the fall. At the point where each leaf stem is attached to a twig, a special layer of cells grows. This blocks the water flow to the leaf by putting a waterproof wall between the leaf and the twig. So when the leaf falls, there's no gaping hole in the twig. There's just a little leaf scar, a new piece of wall to block the hole.

Since the leaves stop calling for water, the roots stop pulling it from the soil. Someone turned off the "faucet" upstairs. Gradually the "pipes" in the trunk drain. When really cold weather arrives, there won't be enough water to freeze and break the "pipes."

If you know exactly what you are going to do in that factory next year, you plan ahead and bring in some supplies. Of course, you have to be careful that whatever you bring can stand the cold temperatures when you turn off the heat. Maybe you bring in some new machinery, but you leave it in boxes. Next spring you will put it together and add the oil and fuel.

That's just what some of those trees do. During the summer they begin to grow next year's leaves. They package those leaves in neat little buds. Then they cover those buds with weather-resistant scales so that next year's machinery will stay safe through the winter.

Suppose that you really like your factory building but are not sure that it will withstand the winter. Maybe it's old and you're afraid that it might collapse this year. What will you do? Well, if you really like its design, you will keep the blueprints in a safe place. You can always build another factory just like this one.

Again, that's just what some of those trees do. They put their last burst of energy into ripening their seeds. Some trees package the seeds in tough nuts which can withstand the winter's cold. Other trees put their seeds into delicious "fruits" which animals and creatures may eat. Either way, the seeds will be safe and will be scattered from the tree. If the winter is really tough and the tree doesn't survive despite its preparations, the seeds are "blueprints" for new trees.

There are differences, of course. Your blueprints are only on paper. The factory you would build would be only bricks and boards. And, of course, the factory you've been thinking about is imaginary.

But those seeds are real. They can sprout into living trees. And those trees we've been talking about are real. They do all the things we've mentioned.

They live and they work. They close up shop for the winter.

And you thought that trees just stood there? Don't be fooled. There's much more going on in creation than you could ever imagine.